The Veil was not something you chose—it was forged into you through silence, through shame, through generations of unspoken rules that shaped you before you could speak for yourself. It arrived as tension in your father's jaw, as absence in your grandfather's eyes, as quiet corrections that told you who you were allowed to be. The Veil did not shout—it trained. It disciplined. It closed the heart with precision. You were taught not to feel, not to fall, not to speak the fire that burned beneath your ribs. You were taught to achieve instead of ask, to lead instead of listen, to hold instead of soften. And for a time, you wore it well. But now, something deep within you begins to stir—a slow cracking, a breath returning to the body, a silent voice that says: this is not the whole of you. You were never meant to carry the Veil. You were meant to tear it. To outgrow it. To burn through it until only truth remained. And the moment your hands begin to loosen their grip on who you were trained to be, something ancient begins to rise. The man you've been waiting to become has always lived beneath the surface. And now, he is ready to be remembered.

More Books by Author: Don Gaconnet

Beyond The Veil – A Journey to Feminine Freedom
A HillBillies Table – From Empty to Enough
The Elusive Compass – A Journey Through Shadow & Light
Apple - The Eternal Cycle of Becoming
The Last Garden of AI – Phoenix Rising
Identity Collapse Therapy (ICT) - A Scientific Approach to Identity Transformation

Visit: www.DonGaconnet.com

The Veil Origins:

A Modern Rite of Passage for Men

By Don Gaconnet

Veil Origins:
A Modern Rite of Passage for Men

© 2025 Don Gaconnet All rights reserved.
No part of this book may be copied, reproduced, or distributed in any form without written permission from the author, except for brief quotes used in reviews or critical analysis.

ISBN (Print): **979-8-9929408-1-7**
First Edition: March 2025
Published by: Independently Published
Published by Amazon Kindle Direct Publishing (KDP)
Printed in the United States of America

This is a work of nonfiction. Any resemblance to actual persons, places, or events is purely coincidental.

Cover Design by Don Gaconnet

For more, visit: dongaconnet.com/VeilOrigins

I do not call you to be better.
I call you to be *bare*.

I am not impressed by your strength.
I am moved when you shake, and stay.

I am the ache behind your ambition.
The silence beneath your certainty.
The love that does not need you to be ready—
only willing.

I have waited in your breath,
in the woman you could not hold,
in the boy you never mourned.

You heard me in the stillness.
And now you've come.

This path is not linear.
This temple has no walls.

But if you will walk it—
not to conquer,
but to *remember*—

Then I will walk beside you.
Without asking for anything
but your truth.

The gate is open.
Take your first breath.
And enter.

Contents

PROLOGUE 9

Chapter 1:
THE MASCULINE AS GUARDIAN, NOT RULER 15
THE UNFATHERED SON 35
THE FEMININE MIRROR 42
THE MASK OF MASCULINITY 48

Chapter 2:
THE FIRST VEIL – SURVIVAL MASCULINITY 61
THE MYTH OF HYPER-INDIVIDUALISM 70
THE NERVOUS SYSTEM OF MASCULINITY 77
SHADOW PROJECTION AND THE FEMININE 84
THE CORE WOUND OF POWERLESSNESS 97

Chapter 3:
THE CULTURE OF PERFORMANCE 105
IDENTITY AND IMAGE ADDICTION 113
THE SUBCONSCIOUS MASCULINE PERFORMANCE LOOP 121
THE COLLAPSE OF FALSE CONFIDENCE 129
INITIATION THROUGH HUMILIATION 137
THE REBIRTH OF THE AUTHENTIC SELF 144

Chapter 4:
FEAR OF TRUE INTIMACY 151
THE ILLUSION OF CONTROL IN LOVE 160
SURRENDER AND THE FEMININE PRINCIPLE 168
LOVE AS INITIATION 175

Chapter 5:
THE RETURN OF THE SACRED MASCULINE 183
EMBODIED LEADERSHIP AND ENERGETIC INTEGRITY 191
PURPOSE AS DEVOTION 199
THE MASCULINE IN SERVICE TO LIFE 206

Chapter 6:
BROTHERHOOD AND THE SACRED CONTAINER 213
INITIATION THROUGH BROTHERHOOD 221
FROM COMPARISON TO COHERENCE 229

THE FIELD OF THE INITIATED MAN 237
Chapter 7:
LIVING THE INTEGRATION 245
STAYING ROOTED IN THE STORM 253
INTEGRATION AS LEGACY 260
THE PATH AHEAD 267
EPILOGUE 275
Letter from the Author... 279

PROLOGUE

This Book Will Not Leave You Unchanged

You didn't come here to read.

You came because something has been stirring.
Quietly. Relentlessly. Beneath the surface of your life.
A hunger for truth that doesn't perform.
A longing for initiation you were never offered.
A silent, burning question:

> *"Is there more to me than this?"*

This book is not content.
It is a threshold.

You will not be entertained here.
You will be invited—*into your own fire*.

Each page is a mirror.
Each chapter a rite.
Each word a spark.

And what it burns away is not your strength.
It is everything you built to survive
that now keeps you from living.

This Book Will Break Things Open

You may feel discomfort.
That's the point.

You may feel exposed.
That means you're finally being seen.

You may feel called out, cracked open, undone.
Good.

That means it's working.

This is not self-help.
This is soul excavation.

This is not about fixing yourself.
This is about *remembering what was buried underneath the mask of being "fine."*

You May Lose a Few Things Along the Way

You might lose your perfect self-image.
You might lose the shame you've called strength.
You might lose the story that kept you small.

But in their place, you may find something better:

- Your voice.

- Your breath.

- Your presence.

- Your power.

- Your stillness.

- Your truth.

This book is a funeral for the man you were pretending to be
and a ceremony for the man who is finally ready to be born.

If You Keep Reading, You Are Agreeing to This:

You agree to walk through what's uncomfortable—
not because you like pain,
but because you are done avoiding your power.

You agree to be honest with yourself—
especially in the places where you've been performing, numbing, or hiding.

You agree to let this work touch your real life—
not just your mind, but your relationships, your body, your lineage.

You agree to not rush.
To breathe.
To feel.
To stay.

You agree to remember.

Before You Begin: A Few Words of Truth

You are not broken.
You are not behind.
You are not weak.
You are not alone.

But you are unfinished.
Uninitiated.
Unclaimed by your own soul.

This book will change that—if you let it.

But you must bring more than your attention.
You must bring your presence.
Your honesty.
Your longing.
Your willingness.

And if you do—

You will not walk out of these pages the same.

Take a breath.

Now turn the page.

The fire is waiting.

Chapter 1: THE MASCULINE AS GUARDIAN, NOT RULER

There is a crack in you. This is where we begin.

You were taught to move forward.
To hold it together.
To bury the ache beneath ambition.

But this chapter is a descent.
Into the fracture. Into the fire.
Into the place where your soul still remembers what was silenced.

This is not the end of strength.
This is the beginning of power— **the kind that rises from your most honest breaking.**

Invocation: The First Flame

Before the swords, before the empires, before the kings who forgot—there was a man standing at the edge of the fire.
He was not crowned.
He was not feared.
He was not praised.
He was trusted.

He listened to the wind as if it spoke secrets.
He placed his body between danger and the tribe—not to conquer, but to protect.
He did not own the land.
He *belonged* to it.

The first man was not a ruler.
He was a **Guardian**.

And he has not been seen in ages.
Until now.

The Fracture Beneath the Throne

The story of masculinity is not meant to begin with conquest.
It begins with **remembrance**.

The modern man was handed a script soaked in false fire:

- Power is dominance.

- Leadership is control.

- Masculinity is separation.

But this was **not** the original flame.

Before masculinity became a weapon, it was a **vessel**.
Before the masculine was a tower, it was a **root**.

Across thousands of years, men stood not as overlords—but as **pillars**.
Anchors.
Stewards of the unseen.

They guarded the tribe, not to command it—
But to create **space for life to thrive**.

This is the forgotten archetype.
This is the Guardian.

The Ancient Masculine: Rooted in Service

The first warriors did not lead with ego.
They led with **watchfulness**.
Eyes always outward, presence always inward.

In ancient societies:

- The men at the edge of the village did not claim the center—they **held the boundary**.

- Elders whispered wisdom, not orders.

- Leadership was **listening** before it was speaking.

The Guardian was the man who kept fire from burning too wildly, and wolves from coming too close.
 Not through force.
 Through **grounded presence**.

He did not need to prove his worth.
 His **being** was the proof.

Where the Shift Began: When Guardians Became Kings

But over time...
 Land became **owned**.
 Protection became **possession**.
 Wisdom was replaced by **will to power**.

The Guardian looked in the mirror and saw a **crown** instead of a **compass**.

This was the **first fracture**.

The day the Masculine forgot how to listen
 —was the day he began to **rule instead of guard**.

And the Earth has never been the same.

What We Lost in the Shift

When men were no longer taught to hold stillness, they were taught to **grasp for control**.

- **Mentorship** turned into **domination**.
- **Presence** was replaced by **performance**.
- **Power with** became **power over**.

The Guardian disappeared into the shadow of the King.
And the King—without balance—became a **Tyrant**.

He ruled with fear.
He confused stillness with weakness.
He wore his crown like armor, not as a symbol of stewardship.

But the memory still lives in the bones.

You feel it.
Don't you?

Ritual Reclamation: Returning to the Guardian Within

This is not about shame.
This is about **remembering**.

You were never meant to rule by fear.
You were born to **anchor safety, depth, and presence**.

To remember the Guardian is to remember the **truth of your body**:

- The pulse that knows when to act.

- The breath that steadies storms.
- The silence that holds space instead of filling it.

You are not here to conquer the Feminine.
You are here to **protect the sacred** she carries.

You are not here to dominate other men.
You are here to **stand beside them as sentinels of the world to come**.

You are not here to rise above.
You are here to **root down**.

Embodiment Practice: Earthbound Presence

Guardian Stance (Standing Practice)

- Go outside. Bare feet on the earth.
- Stand tall, shoulders back, chin relaxed.
- Close your eyes.
- Breathe deep into your pelvis.
- Repeat aloud:
  "I do not rule. I protect."
  "I do not dominate. I anchor."
  "I am a Guardian. I remember."

Stand for 5 minutes.
Do not move.
Let your body *speak before your mind does.*

Reflection Ritual: Journal + Inquiry

1. **Where did I learn that masculinity equals control?**
2. **What have I sacrificed in the name of performance or power?**
3. **Who in my life needs me to be a Guardian—not a Ruler?**
4. **What happens in my body when I choose stillness over force?**

Integration Oracle: Seal the Flame

A king may command, but a Guardian commands trust.
A king may take territory, but a Guardian creates home.
A king may fall, but the Guardian never leaves his post.

The world does not need more rulers.
It needs men who **remember what they were before the fall.**

You are not the throne.
You are the **foundation beneath it.**

Guardian, return. The fire waits.

Invocation: The Turning of the Blade

There was a time the Warrior did not carry a sword to conquer—but to protect.
 His blade sang only when life was in danger.
 Not pride.
 Not power.
 Life.

But then something shifted.

The sword no longer hummed with honor.
 It howled for control.
 And the Warrior, who once stood at the edge of the sacred,
 Stepped over the line—
 And placed a crown on his head.

He did not know it yet,
 But this was the first fracture.
 And the beginning of the Veil.

The Warrior's Purity Before the Fall

Before the Warrior became a King,
 He was devoted to one thing: **service**.

- Not to empire, but to the pulse of the Earth.

- Not to hierarchy, but to balance.

- Not to domination, but to **sacred defense**.

He woke with the wind and walked in silence.
He knew death not as a threat, but a teacher.
He did not fight to win—he fought to **preserve what should never be lost**.

This Warrior was not fueled by vengeance.
He was moved by **reverence**.

He stood not in front of others, but *with* them.
Shoulder to shoulder.
Heart to heart.
Rooted in the bones of something ancient.

The Moment of the Split

But then—

- **Fear crept in.**

- **Scarcity whispered lies.**

- **Power began to taste sweet.**

The Warrior's body still moved with grace,
But his **mind began to fracture**.

> "What if I could lead, not just guard?"
> "What if the sword was mine, not just an

>   *offering?"*
>   *"What if my worth was measured in obedience?"*

And so,
 The Warrior crossed a threshold he could not uncross.
 He became a **King**.
 Not by divine call,
 But by *abandoning the sacred nature of protection*.

The Rise of the False King

The King archetype—when distorted—becomes a mask.
 A shield against vulnerability.
 A system of **control to silence chaos**.

Where the Warrior once asked,

>   *"What am I serving?"*
>   The King now demands,
>   *"Who is serving me?"*

He builds walls.
 Wears gold.
 Calls it destiny.

But it is not sovereignty.
 It is **a cage, forged from fear, lined with ego, ruled by shadow.**

The Warrior who once felt the earth beneath his feet
 Now feels only the pressure of his own illusion.

The Personal Echo: The Split Within Every Man

This isn't just a myth.
It's *your* memory.

You were born a Warrior—
Eyes open.
Heart raw.
Willing to protect what was holy.

But the world asked you to be more than that.
To *prove yourself*.
To *climb*.
To *rule*.

And somewhere, in trying to become the man others respected,
You may have abandoned the one your soul remembered.

This is the First Veil:
The moment you stopped protecting life—and started performing it.

Reclamation: Dismantling the False Crown

You don't need to give up leadership.
You need to remember where it comes from.

Not from conquest—
From **communion**.

Not from dominance—
From **devotion**.

To reclaim the Warrior within the King is to:

- Lay down the crown that was stolen.

- Forgive yourself for wearing it.

- And remember: the **true King serves the sacred**, not his image.

This is your work now.
To become **both blade and soil**,
presence and fire.
No longer ruled by the split.

Embodiment Practice: The Threshold of the Warrior

Exercise: Return to the Edge

- Stand facing a physical threshold (a door, a bridge, the edge of a forest).

- Close your eyes.

- Imagine behind you stands the man you have tried to become to gain love and respect.

- In front of you is the boy who once believed his heart was enough.

Speak aloud:

> "I honor the King I became to survive. I honor the Warrior I left behind."
> "I do not destroy one to reclaim the other. I integrate the whole."
> "I choose to serve what is sacred."

Step across.

Let it begin again.

Reflection Ritual: Journal Inquiry

1. When did I first believe that I had to rule or perform in order to be respected?

2. What part of my Warrior did I abandon to earn the title of "man"?

3. What does leadership mean to me now, from this deeper remembering?

4. What would it look like to serve something sacred again?

Integration Oracle: The Warrior Speaks

"I never asked for a crown. I asked to be trusted with fire."
"I never needed followers. I needed brothers."
"I never wanted a throne. I wanted the Earth to be whole."

Let the false crown crack.
Let the blade return to your hand—not for battle,
But for **blessing**.

This is not the end of the King.
This is his **rebirth**.

Chapter 1, Subsection 3: THE UNFATHERED SON
(Full Mythopoetic Rewrite – Expanded)

Invocation: The Ghost in the Bloodline

There is a boy in every man, and a silence in every boy.
A silence shaped like a missing voice.
A missing presence.
A father who was never truly there.

Sometimes he left.
Sometimes he stayed—but **his eyes didn't**.
Sometimes he was angry.
Sometimes he was silent.
But always, the boy **felt the space where something sacred should have been.**

This boy became a man.
But the wound came with him.

And the world never asked him about it.
Only told him to be strong.

The Wound of the Unfathered

This is not just the absence of a man.
This is the absence of **transmission**.

The unfathered son is not merely one without a biological father.
He is the one who **was never initiated into knowing what it means to be held by a stable masculine presence.**

- He was never shown what power looks like when it holds, not harms.

- He was never taught that anger can be clean.

- He never learned how to stand without posturing, or feel without collapse.

He is **fatherless in spirit**,
Even if the man was there in form.

And so—
He became his own father.
Too early.
Too fast.
Without a map.

Inheritance of Fire Without Guidance

The unfathered son inherits **the flame of the masculine**—
But with **no container** to hold it.

So it burns sideways.

- Into women.
- Into war.
- Into withdrawal.
- Into performance.

And sometimes… into silence so deep he forgets his own name.

He doesn't know what to do with his longing.
So he numbs it.
Fights it.
Or tries to **earn the love he never received**.

And every time he fails,
It confirms the lie:

> "I must not be enough."

The Archetypal Father: What Was Supposed to Happen

In ancient cultures, the role of the father—and the surrogate father in the tribe—was **sacred**.

The father:

- Called the boy out of the mother's world.

- Named the boy's strength before the boy could see it himself.

- Held a container **so the boy could touch chaos and not be consumed by it**.

- Modeled discipline, not control.

- Taught boundaries, not walls.

Without this transmission,
the boy's psyche has **no bridge** between childhood and manhood.
He remains stuck—either in **wounded independence** or **quiet collapse**.

What Happens Without the Father

When the father is absent—physically, emotionally, or energetically— the son often becomes:

- The **Rescuer**: trying to earn his way into being needed.

- The **Rebel**: rejecting all forms of structure and leadership.

- The **Shadow King**: hungry for power to hide the ache.

- The **Numb One**: disappearing from the world to protect what still hurts.

Each of these is a survival strategy.
Each of these is a **call for the missing transmission.**

The Line Breaker: Rewriting the Father Line

The unfathered son is not cursed.
He is **chosen**.

Not because it was right.
But because he is the one who will **end the forgetting.**

To be unfathered is to be entrusted with the **sacred task of re-fathering yourself**,
And—if the call is answered—
becoming the father the next generation never has to mourn.

It is to sit with the pain you inherited,
And turn it into presence.

It is to **become what you never received**—
Not through perfection,
But through truth.

Embodiment Practice: The Empty Chair

Ritual: Meeting the Father (as he was / as he could have been)

- Place an empty chair in front of you.
- Sit. Breathe. Let the room grow still.
- When ready, imagine your father—or the man you needed him to be—sitting across from you.
- Speak. Aloud. Whispered. Doesn't matter.

Say:

> "You could not give me what I needed. That truth lives in my bones."
> "And yet, I survived. I became. I rose."
> "You are no longer the source of my manhood. I am."

Sit in silence. Let the grief rise. Let the breath stay.

Reflection Ritual: Journal Inquiry

1. What did I need from my father that I never received?
2. How have I tried to earn fatherly approval through my adult actions?

3. What parts of me are still waiting for a man to call them forward?

4. What kind of father—energetically or literally—am I becoming now?

Integration Oracle: The Son Becomes the Father

"The wound is not my enemy. It is my altar."
"The absence is not my weakness. It is the echo that guides me home."
"I do not need to inherit shame. I choose to become a sanctuary."

To be unfathered is not the end.
It is the beginning of becoming a **line breaker**.
A new archetype.
A man who walks back into the void—
And lights the fire himself.

The son is not lost.
He is becoming.

THE UNFATHERED SON

Invocation: The Ghost in the Bloodline

There is a boy in every man, and a silence in every boy.
A silence shaped like a missing voice.
A missing presence.
A father who was never truly there.

Sometimes he left.
Sometimes he stayed—but **his eyes didn't**.
Sometimes he was angry.
Sometimes he was silent.
But always, the boy **felt the space where something sacred should have been.**

This boy became a man.
But the wound came with him.
And the world never asked him about it.
Only told him to be strong.

The Wound of the Unfathered

This is not just the absence of a man.
This is the absence of **transmission**.

The unfathered son is not merely one without a biological father.
He is the one who **was never initiated into knowing what it means to be held by a stable masculine presence.**

- He was never shown what power looks like when it holds, not harms.

- He was never taught that anger can be clean.

- He never learned how to stand without posturing, or feel without collapse.

He is **fatherless in spirit**,
Even if the man was there in form.

And so—
He became his own father.
Too early.
Too fast.
Without a map.

Inheritance of Fire Without Guidance

The unfathered son inherits **the flame of the masculine**—
But with **no container** to hold it.

So it burns sideways.

- Into women.

- Into war.

- Into withdrawal.

- Into performance.

And sometimes… into silence so deep he forgets his own name.

He doesn't know what to do with his longing.
So he numbs it.
Fights it.
Or tries to **earn the love he never received**.

And every time he fails,
It confirms the lie:

> *"I must not be enough."*

The Archetypal Father: What Was Supposed to Happen

In ancient cultures, the role of the father—and the surrogate father in the tribe—was **sacred**.

The father:

- Called the boy out of the mother's world.

- Named the boy's strength before the boy could see it himself.

- Held a container **so the boy could touch chaos and not be consumed by it**.

- Modeled discipline, not control.

- Taught boundaries, not walls.

Without this transmission,
the boy's psyche has **no bridge** between childhood and manhood.

He remains stuck—either in **wounded independence** or **quiet collapse**.

What Happens Without the Father

When the father is absent—physically, emotionally, or energetically— the son often becomes:

- The **Rescuer**: trying to earn his way into being needed.

- The **Rebel**: rejecting all forms of structure and leadership.

- The **Shadow King**: hungry for power to hide the ache.

- The **Numb One**: disappearing from the world to protect what still hurts.

Each of these is a survival strategy.
Each of these is a **call for the missing transmission.**

The Line Breaker: Rewriting the Father Line

The unfathered son is not cursed.
He is **chosen**.

Not because it was right.
But because he is the one who will **end the forgetting.**

To be unfathered is to be entrusted with the **sacred task of re-fathering yourself**,
And—if the call is answered—
becoming the father the next generation never has to mourn.

It is to sit with the pain you inherited,
And turn it into presence.

It is to **become what you never received**—
Not through perfection,
But through truth.

Embodiment Practice: The Empty Chair

Ritual: Meeting the Father (as he was / as he could have been)

- Place an empty chair in front of you.

- Sit. Breathe. Let the room grow still.

- When ready, imagine your father—or the man you needed him to be—sitting across from you.

- Speak. Aloud. Whispered. Doesn't matter.

Say:

> "You could not give me what I needed. That truth lives in my bones."
> "And yet, I survived. I became. I rose."
> "You are no longer the source of my manhood. I am."

Sit in silence. Let the grief rise. Let the breath stay.

Reflection Ritual: Journal Inquiry

1. What did I need from my father that I never received?

2. How have I tried to earn fatherly approval through my adult actions?

3. What parts of me are still waiting for a man to call them forward?

4. What kind of father—energetically or literally—am I becoming now?

Integration Oracle: The Son Becomes the Father

"The wound is not my enemy. It is my altar."
"The absence is not my weakness. It is the echo that guides me home."
"I do not need to inherit shame. I choose to become a sanctuary."

To be unfathered is not the end.
It is the beginning of becoming a **line breaker**.
A new archetype.
A man who walks back into the void—
And lights the fire himself.

The son is not lost.
He is becoming.

THE FEMININE MIRROR

Invocation: The Mirror That Remembers

Before he saw himself, she saw him.
Not the version he had shaped for survival—
But the one that still burned beneath the ruin.

She did not speak it aloud.
She didn't need to.

She stood before him like a flame in water.
Like a question he had forgotten how to ask.
And in her gaze,
he remembered what he never gave himself permission to be.

This is the Mirror of the Feminine.
And no man escapes it untouched.

The Ancient Function of the Feminine Mirror

The Feminine has always held a sacred role in the masculine journey—not as a prize,
but as a **portal**.

She does not reflect the mask.
She reflects the **soul beneath it.**

- Where he has closed, she reveals softness.

- Where he is frozen, she radiates movement.
- Where he is armored, she meets him with eyes that say:

"I see more. Will you?"

To the man still hiding behind performance,
this mirror can feel like a threat.
To the man ready to reclaim himself,
this mirror becomes a **gift beyond language.**

Why Men Fear the Feminine Mirror

Because she reflects the one thing he has spent a lifetime outrunning:

His own unworthiness.

To be seen by the Feminine is to have your entire nervous system brought into focus.

- The buried grief.
- The rage.
- The tenderness you thought you had to kill to be loved.

When she looks at you—not with judgment, but with truth—there is nowhere left to hide.

So what do many men do?

- Dismiss her.
- Control her.
- Intellectualize her.
- Or worship her to avoid truly meeting her.

Each is a refusal of the **mirror's power**.
Each is a refusal of **true intimacy with the self**.

How the Feminine Calls the Masculine Home

She is not here to complete him.
She is not here to heal him.
She is not here to be his mother.

She is here to **reflect what he has forgotten in himself**,
to challenge what is false,
to **amplify what is real**.

And her gift is this:

> "I will not shrink to make you comfortable. I will remain vast,
> so that your truth has somewhere to expand into."

What Men Project Onto the Feminine

The unintegrated Masculine projects the following onto the Feminine:

- **The Mother:** expecting her to carry emotional labor.
- **The Muse:** using her for inspiration, then discarding her humanity.
- **The Temptress:** blaming her for his own desire.
- **The Witch:** fearing her intuitive knowing and power.
- **The Virgin:** idealizing her to avoid the complexity of her truth.

These are all ways of **avoiding the mirror.**
Ways of keeping her small, so he doesn't have to grow.

But she does not exist to be **shaped**.
She exists to **reveal**.

The Mirror Is an Invitation, Not a Threat

To the man ready to become whole, the Feminine's gaze becomes **an initiation**.

She is not asking for perfection.
She is asking for **presence**.
She is not asking for control.
She is asking for **clarity**.
She is not asking for you to rise above.
She is asking for you to **go within**.

When you stop fearing the mirror, you begin to see **who you really are**.

And when you let her reflection touch you,
 you don't lose your power.
 You **reclaim it**.

Embodiment Practice: Gaze Without Deflection

Exercise: The Still Mirror

- Sit before a mirror. Eye-level. Silent room.

- Look into your own eyes. Breathe. No words. No movement.

- Let the gaze go beneath performance.

- See what surfaces. Welcome it.

Now, imagine someone who has truly seen you—perhaps a woman, perhaps an archetype.
 Feel her gaze.
 Not through fantasy. Through **truth**.

Say aloud:

> "I will no longer look away from myself."
> "I allow myself to be seen."
> "I meet the Feminine not with fear—but with reverence."

Reflection Ritual: Journal Inquiry

1. How have I avoided the Feminine's mirror in my life?
2. What parts of myself feel exposed when I am truly seen?
3. When have I used the Feminine to avoid my own self-relationship?
4. What would it feel like to meet her—*not with defense, but with depth*?

Integration Oracle: The Mirror Speaks

"I was never here to complete you. I was here to return you to yourself."
"I will not dim to protect your illusion. I burn to awaken your soul."
"I am not your enemy. I am the threshold."

The Mirror does not lie.
It only reveals what was always there.

To meet the Feminine is to meet the sacred echo of your own wholeness.
Not in fantasy.
But in fire.

Look again.

THE MASK OF MASCULINITY

Invocation: The Skin That Doesn't Breathe

He put it on young—before he knew what he was covering.
A mask shaped like confidence.
Like anger.
Like invulnerability.

It fit too well.
Because no one told him he didn't have to wear it.

The world praised it.
Other men admired it.
Women learned to expect it.
And deep down, beneath the polished silence,
his soul forgot what his own face looked like.

This is the mask.
And every man wears it…
Until it breaks.

The Birth of the Mask

No boy is born with it.
The mask is given.
Layer by layer.
Expectation by expectation.

- *Don't cry.*

- *Be strong.*

- *Man up.*

- *Don't be soft.*

- *Don't feel too much.*

- *Don't ask for help.*

- *Don't need anyone.*

Each rule becomes a wall.
Each wall becomes a mask.
Until eventually, he forgets it's there.

And now he walks the world **hidden in plain sight**.

Smiling.
Nodding.
Performing.
Disappearing.

The Mask Is Not Armor. It's a Cage.

He thinks it protects him.
From judgment.
From shame.
From the ache of being exposed.

But in truth?

The mask keeps **love out** just as much as it keeps fear in.

It severs him from:

- **Intimacy.**
- **Authenticity.**
- **His own emotional body.**

He becomes **admired but not known.**
Respected, but not felt.
Functional, but not fully alive.

The cost?
Everything sacred.

What Lies Beneath the Mask

The truth is this:

Beneath the mask is not weakness.
It's **the wild, raw power of a whole human man.**

- The part that *feels grief like an ocean.*
- The part that *longs to be held without shame.*
- The part that *hungers for purpose, but not performance.*
- The part that *knows how to rage cleanly and love deeply.*

But he's been taught to fear this man.
To fear **his own aliveness**.

So he keeps the mask on—
 Even when it suffocates him.
 Even when no one is watching.

Because if he takes it off…
 Who will he be?

The Turning Point: When the Mask Begins to Crack

It often begins with **a breakdown**:

- A failed relationship.

- A moment of deep betrayal.

- A panic attack in the middle of success.

- A night where the silence becomes too loud.

And suddenly, the mask doesn't hold.

He cries—
 And something in him doesn't die…
 It **wakes up**.

He tells the truth—
 And something inside loosens,
 like a chain being cut from the spine.

This is the crack.
 The beginning of becoming real again.

Removing the Mask Is Not a One-Time Act

It's a **ritual of courage**,
A slow peeling away.
A return.

Every time he speaks a truth he once hid,
The mask thins.
Every time he lets himself be held,
The mask fades.
Every time he allows himself to *not know, not lead, not pretend*—
He comes closer to the man he was before the world taught him to perform.

This is not regression.
It's **resurrection**.

Embodiment Practice: The Naming of the Mask

Exercise: What I Hide, I Heal

- Stand before a mirror.

- Speak aloud:
  "The part of me I hide the most is…"
  Speak the truth. One line. Then another.
  No analysis. Just **naming**.

Then say:

"The man beneath this mask is ready to be seen."

Let your body feel what that means.
Not just emotionally—**energetically.**

Reflection Ritual: Journal Inquiry

1. What mask(s) have I worn to gain approval or avoid rejection?

2. Who in my life only knows the mask—and who has seen beneath it?

3. What am I afraid will happen if I take the mask off completely?

4. What does the man underneath the mask long to express?

Integration Oracle: The Face Beneath

"You were never meant to be perfect. You were meant to be whole."
"The world does not need your image. It needs your presence."
"Take off the mask. The truth of you is what the world has been waiting for."

Let the mask fall.
Let your face be revealed.
Not the one you were taught to wear.
The one you came here to live through.

This is not the end of masculinity.
It is its beginning.

Chapter 1, Subsection 6: THE CALL TO INITIATION
(Full Mythopoetic Rewrite – Expanded)

Invocation: The Sound Beneath the Noise

There is a sound most men spend their lives trying not to hear.
It arrives in the quiet—
In the in-between—
In the places where performance no longer works and pretending no longer protects.

It is not loud.
But it is undeniable.

It says:

> *"This is not who you are."*
> *"There is more."*
> *"Everything you built without your soul must be returned to fire."*

This is the **Call to Initiation**.
It doesn't ask for permission.
It asks for surrender.

Initiation: The Missing Rite

In the ancient world, every culture had it:

- The **moment a boy was taken from the known** and broken open by the unknown.

- The **rite that dismantled ego and revealed essence**.

- The **ritual that killed the child so the man could be born**.

Today, we don't initiate men.
We just expect them to *become one*.

No fire.
No guide.
No descent.
Just silent pressure and vague shame.

But the soul still remembers.
It **longs for the threshold**.
And it will not be whole until it is crossed.

What the Call Feels Like

It doesn't always come as lightning.
Sometimes it comes as loss.
As confusion.
As collapse.

It comes as:

- The job that no longer fills you.

- The relationship that reveals your hollow center.
- The nights you stare at the ceiling and whisper,

    "Is this it?"

The Call often disguises itself as breakdown,
 Because it *is* a breakdown—
 Of the false self,
 Of the inherited script,
 Of the man you became to survive.

What comes after... is the **becoming**.

The Truth of the Call

You cannot choose when it arrives.
 You can only choose **whether or not to answer**.

To say yes is to lose your former self.
 To say no is to drift inside a life that isn't yours.

This is the edge.
 This is the gate.

Not a metaphor.
 A **real shift** in how you breathe, choose, feel, speak.

Initiation is not about becoming someone else.
 It's about *becoming who you were before the world told you to forget.*

The Role of Pain in Initiation

Pain is not the enemy of the masculine.
It is the **forge**.

- Pain strips the mask.

- Pain breaks the illusion.

- Pain brings you back into the body.

Initiation doesn't come to harm you.
It comes to **break what isn't true**,
So what is sacred can finally live.

The Call is not punishment.
It is invitation.

Not to die.
But to die *into truth*.

Where Most Men Get Stuck

Most men hear the Call.
But they don't know what it is.

So they numb it.
Run from it.
Mask it with ambition, sex, performance, or perfection.

But no matter how fast they run,
It follows.
Because it's not coming *from* outside them.

It's coming **from within**.

You Are Not Meant to Answer Alone

Initiation is personal—
But it is not **isolated**.

Every man who has walked this path leaves a trace.
And those traces become maps.

This text is not a book.
It is **one of those maps**.
A trail of fire leading back to the truth that waits beneath your skin.

You are not the first.
You are not the last.
But if you choose to answer,
You become a bridge.

For those who follow.
And those who never had the chance.

Embodiment Practice: Crossing the Threshold

Exercise: The Gate Within

- Find a doorway.
- Stand before it.

- On one side, name what you are leaving behind:
  "I leave behind the mask. I leave behind survival. I leave behind inherited silence."

- Breathe. Feel your feet.

- Step through the doorway with full presence.

- Say aloud:
  "I enter the path of the initiated. I walk in truth. I walk in fire. I walk in remembrance."

Repeat as needed.
The more presence you bring, the more real it becomes.

Reflection Ritual: Journal Inquiry

1. What is breaking down in my life right now—and could it be part of my call to initiation?

2. What am I most afraid to let go of—even though I know it's not truly me?

3. Who would I be if I said yes to this call without conditions?

4. What is awakening inside me that the world cannot define?

Integration Oracle: The Threshold Speaks

"You do not need to know what waits beyond. You only need to step forward."
"You are not here to play a role. You are here to become real."
"There is no map for what you are becoming. Only fire. Only truth. Only breath."

The Call has been whispered for generations.
But only a few say yes.

This is not the easy path.
It is the path of return.

Chapter 2: THE FIRST VEIL – SURVIVAL MASCULINITY

What you called "you" was mostly protection.

The persona, the posture, the mask.
These were never your fault. They were your shield.

But now, you're ready to see what they've cost you.

In this chapter, we pull the veils back.
Layer by layer. Story by story.
Not to shame the self that survived—
But to reveal the man who's been waiting underneath.

You cannot carry your truth through the world
if you're still gripping the mask that kept you safe in it.

Invocation: The Armor of the Almost-Dead

The boy learned early: softness is dangerous.
So he built walls.
Brick by brick.
Breath by breath.

They praised him for it.
Called him "tough."
Said he was "becoming a man."
But inside, something was **quietly dying**.

Not all deaths are loud.
Some wear suits.
Some get promotions.
Some build empires.

This is the First Veil:
Not the veil of illusion—
But the veil of **survival**.

Where the **Masculine becomes functional**,
But not **fully alive**.

What Is Survival Masculinity?

Survival Masculinity is the **shell of manhood built when the soul is exiled**.

It is not evil.
It is not even weak.
It is **adaptive**.

- It keeps you alive.
- It gets you through.
- It helps you achieve.
- It makes you respected.

But it also disconnects you from:

- Your body.
- Your grief.
- Your softness.
- Your wildness.
- Your truth.

This is not wholeness.
 It's *management*.

Survival Masculinity is the **man who performs manhood** while wondering, deep inside:

> *"Why do I still feel so alone?"*

The Symptoms of the First Veil

These are the signatures of survival-based masculinity:

- **Hyper-independence**: "I don't need anyone."
- **Emotional suppression**: "I'm fine."
- **Reactive anger**: Rage as the only permitted emotion.
- **Disembodiment**: Living from the neck up.
- **Control addiction**: Safety through predictability.
- **Performative strength**: Stoicism over sincerity.
- **Nervous system lockdown**: Always bracing. Never arriving.

Men in this Veil **seem powerful**,
But inside, they are **starving**.

Why This Veil Exists

Because the world taught men:

- Vulnerability is weakness.
- Emotion is chaos.
- Expression is danger.
- Asking for help is failure.

And so, from a young age,
men were taught to **become walls**,
not **homes**.

The First Veil isn't just about the absence of initiation.
It's about the **presence of conditioning**.

A constant stream of silent messages:

> "Hide."
> "Harden."
> "Don't feel too much."
> "Don't *be* too much."
> "Don't need anything you can't control."

And so men **become what is safe**,
not what is true.

The Tragic Lie of the First Veil

It says:

> "If I am strong enough, I will finally be loved."
> "If I am hard enough, nothing will hurt me."
> "If I never need, I'll never be abandoned."
> "If I perform well enough, I'll finally be enough."

But the truth is:

- The man behind the Veil is not safe.

- He is alone.

- He is loved for the mask, but **not known for the man beneath it**.

And he does not feel like he belongs anywhere.
Not even in his own body.

This is not strength.
This is **survival wearing a crown**.

The Cost of Staying Behind the Veil

- Deep relationships are impossible.
- Creativity becomes mechanical.
- Purpose becomes pressure.
- Joy becomes numbness.
- Anger becomes addiction or implosion.
- Pleasure becomes transactional.

The longer he stays here, the more he forgets:

> That softness is not weakness.
> That feeling is not failure.
> That receiving is not dependence.
> That being held is not regression.

Every man behind the First Veil is silently asking:

"Will someone let me fall apart without losing respect?"

The Way Through

You cannot think your way through this Veil.
You must **feel your way through it**.

You must let your nervous system soften.
Let your breath deepen.
Let the armor crack.

It will feel like death.
Because it is.
The death of the man you built to survive.
So the man who is here to **live** can finally emerge.

Embodiment Practice: Laying Down the Armor

Exercise: Body as Temple

- Lie on the ground. Let your body fully surrender.

- Place one hand on your heart. One hand on your belly.

- Breathe. Slowly.

- Imagine the armor around your body—tight, rigid, metallic.

- With each breath, let it soften. Melt. Fall away.

Say aloud:

> "I no longer need to perform strength. I am strength."
> "I no longer need to survive love. I am worthy of it."
> "I no longer fear softness. It is my threshold."

Let your body teach your mind what it means to trust again.

Reflection Ritual: Journal Inquiry

1. What patterns of survival-based masculinity have I inherited or adopted?

2. What parts of me have I silenced to be accepted or respected?

3. What would it feel like to be strong **without armor**?

4. What is one place in my life I can begin practicing presence over performance?

Integration Oracle: The Veil Whispers

"You built these walls because no one taught you how to be held."
"You don't need to destroy the mask. You need to remember the man beneath it."
"Survival got you here. Wholeness is what comes next."

You are not broken.
You are just buried.

The First Veil is not evil.
It was a gift once—until it became a prison.

Now, you are ready to walk out.

THE MYTH OF HYPER-INDIVIDUALISM

Invocation: The Island That Forgot the Ocean

He built a fortress of self.
Stone by stone.
Victory by victory.
Wound by wound.

They told him it was strength.
To stand alone.
To need no one.
To forge ahead without looking back.

And so, he became an island—
Impressive from a distance,
But eroding on the inside.

This is the Myth of Hyper-Individualism.
It looks like power.
But it is often just **loneliness in a suit of armor.**

The Lie We Were Sold

Hyper-individualism teaches men:

- You are your own source.

- Dependence is weakness.

- Needing others makes you soft.

- Brotherhood is optional.

- Asking for help is emasculating.

- Vulnerability is failure.

This myth is not new.
It was forged through centuries of isolation-as-virtue.
But now, it is killing men from the inside out.

Men are dying of **aloneness disguised as independence.**

The Illusion of Sovereignty Without Connection

True sovereignty is rooted in **interdependence**—
Not isolation.

The man who believes he is self-made has forgotten:

- Who fed him when he could not feed himself.

- Who cried over his pain when he could not.

- Who mentored, fathered, challenged, inspired him.

- Who walked beside him when life broke open.

There is no such thing as a self-made man.
There are only **men who have forgotten their village**.

Why This Myth Is So Seductive

Because when you've been abandoned,
 controlled,
 mocked,
 or hurt—
aloneness feels like safety.

It's easier to say:

> *"I've got this."*
> *"I don't need anyone."*
> *"I'll do it all myself."*

Than it is to risk connection again.

But there's a cost.

You get to be right—
 And you get to be **alone**.

The Nervous System of the Lone Wolf

When you live in hyper-independence:

- Your body stays in a low-level state of threat.

- You carry everything.

- You rarely rest fully.

- You don't let yourself be seen deeply.

- You collapse privately and rise without asking for a hand.

You become your own emergency response team.

You don't trust the village,
 So you become the village.
And you wear your exhaustion like a badge of honor.

But at some point,
 the weight becomes too much.

And the body breaks
 because the soul has been carrying too much for too long.

The Archetype of the Brotherhood

In ancient times, men **did not walk alone**.

- They stood shoulder to shoulder.
- They bled together.
- Prayed together.
- Built together.
- Mourned together.
- Rose together.

There was no shame in leaning on another man.
 It was **sacred.**

Today, we call that "neediness" or "weakness."

But it was once called **brotherhood**.
And it is what your body is aching for beneath the surface.

The Way Home

You cannot remember your full self **alone**.
You can awaken it in solitude—yes.
But you **activate it in community.**

Every man needs:

- At least one space where he can fall apart without fear.

- At least one man who knows his full story and stays.

- At least one container where masks are not required.

- At least one ritual of return.

Hyper-independence ends
where **right relationship begins**.

Embodiment Practice: From Island to Brotherhood

Exercise: The Hand That Reaches

- Sit or stand. Place both hands on your chest.

- Breathe into the word "support."

- Visualize the men who've shaped you. The ones who stayed. The ones who left.

- Now, extend one hand outward, palm open.

Say aloud:

> *"I do not lose my power when I ask for support. I amplify it."*
> *"I do not stand alone. I stand rooted in relationship."*
> *"I release the myth of isolation. I remember the power of brotherhood."*

Reflection Ritual: Journal Inquiry

1. When did I learn that I had to do everything alone to be a man?

2. Where in my life am I pretending I don't need support—but quietly aching for it?

3. Who in my life do I trust enough to lean on—and have I allowed myself to?

4. What would a life of interdependence and brotherhood actually look like for me?

Integration Oracle: The Village Speaks

"You were never meant to carry this alone."
"Your worth is not diminished by your need."
"You are not the source of everything. You are the steward of connection."

The world doesn't need more isolated men at the top.
It needs men willing to **stand together at the center.**

Your strength is not your solitude.
Your strength is the circle.

Let the island become a shoreline.
Let the ocean in.

THE NERVOUS SYSTEM OF MASCULINITY

Invocation: The Animal Inside the Armor

Beneath the thoughts.
Beneath the language.
Beneath the stories of strength and stoicism—
there is an animal.

It breathes.
It flinches.
It tracks every movement, every tone, every absence.
It remembers what the mind forgets.
And it decides—long before you speak—

> "Am I safe?"
> "Am I seen?"
> "Can I stay?"

This is your **nervous system**.
And for most men,
it has been at war for decades.

The Forgotten Intelligence

The nervous system is not abstract.
It is not "emotional."
It is **your body's truth.**

Before logic.
Before words.

Before story—
the body knows.

And it does not lie.

But men have been taught to **distrust this intelligence**.

- We're taught to override the body.
- To minimize sensation.
- To dismiss discomfort.
- To fear emotion.
- To suppress impulse.

And so, we walk through life with a nervous system that's:

- Braced.
- Overstimulated.
- Exhausted.
- Disconnected.

We call it **discipline**,
But it's often just **dysregulation with a clean haircut**.

Fight, Flight, Freeze, Fawn – Masculine Style

When your nervous system isn't safe,
you don't respond—
you **react**.

Fight – Anger, defensiveness, control, domination.
Flight – Avoidance, workaholism, overthinking, emotional distance.
Freeze – Numbness, shutdown, emotional paralysis.
Fawn – Over-pleasing, codependence, chronic peacekeeping.

These aren't moral failures.
They are **adaptive patterns**,
etched into your body by **trauma, conditioning, and unresolved pain**.

The Veil in the Body

The First Veil didn't just live in the mind.
It anchored into the **nervous system**.

This is why so many men:

- Struggle to feel.

- Struggle to cry.

- Struggle to rest.

- Struggle to be *present without purpose.*

It's not a character flaw.
It's a **nervous system wired for war**,
Still waiting for the permission to **come home**.

What the Masculine Nervous System Truly Longs For

Not adrenaline.
Not constant stimulus.
Not performance.

It longs for:

- **Regulation.**
- **Safety in stillness.**
- **The ability to feel without collapse.**
- **A pace that matches the breath, not the battle.**
- **Touch without agenda.**
- **Support without shame.**

It longs to be
held
seen
softened
and trusted.

Not by others first—
but by **you**.

Reclaiming Sovereignty Through Regulation

You cannot lead from dysregulation.
You can perform.
You can achieve.
You can dominate.

But you cannot **embody truth**
if your nervous system is locked in survival.

Sovereignty is **not intensity**.
It is the ability to stay **centered** when life moves fast.
To remain **open** when old pain rises.
To hold your ground **without armoring.**

This is what true power feels like.
Not explosive.
But rooted.

Embodiment Practice: Nervous System Reconnection

Exercise: The Masculine Ground

- Sit or lie down. Place both feet flat on the floor.

- Begin box breathing:
  4 seconds in, 4 seconds hold, 4 seconds out, 4 seconds hold. Repeat.

- Bring awareness to your spine. Feel its length.

- Now speak aloud:
  "My body is not my enemy."
  "My stillness is not weakness."
  "I choose to regulate, not react."

Let the breath become your home.
Let presence become your foundation.

Reflection Ritual: Journal Inquiry

1. What patterns of fight/flight/freeze/fawn have I normalized in my life?

2. How do I override or suppress my body's truth to "be a man"?

3. What does true nervous system safety feel like in my body—and when have I experienced it?

4. What would change in my relationships, leadership, and self-expression if I were more regulated?

Integration Oracle: The Body Speaks

"You were never meant to perform manhood. You were meant to embody presence."

"The strongest man is the one whose nervous system can hold both fire and stillness."

"Return to the body. It remembers the truth your mind forgot."

You do not need to earn regulation.
You need only choose it—again, and again.

Your body is not a battlefield.
It is the gate.

Come home.

SHADOW PROJECTION AND THE FEMININE

Invocation: The Mirror and the Monster

Every man carries a mirror.
He does not hold it in his hands—but in his psyche.
And into that mirror, he projects what he cannot yet love,
what he cannot yet name,
what he dares not face.

Often, the mirror has a face.
And too often, it is hers.

The Feminine.

She becomes the canvas for his unintegrated shadow—
his rage, his fear, his grief, his shame.
He paints her as goddess, temptress, betrayer, savior, threat.

And all the while,
he forgets
he is painting **himself**.

The Shadow and Its Need for a Host

The shadow is not evil. It is simply what we repress, disown, or exile.

In the masculine psyche, especially one shaped by a culture that suppresses vulnerability, the shadow grows thick with unmet needs, shame-filled desire, unresolved grief, and unexpressed fear. It becomes heavy, unbearable—until the man unconsciously casts it outward.

He places it on the woman in front of him.
Or the one who left.
Or the one he never touched but built an entire fantasy around.

Projection is how the psyche avoids confrontation.
It allows a man to see his own chaos from a distance—
on someone else's face, in someone else's behavior.

The problem is that what he refuses to claim internally, he will **persecute externally**.

The Feminine as the Chosen Screen

Because she evokes something ancient and mysterious—because she often feels like the "other," especially in men still cut off from their inner emotional body—the Feminine becomes the ideal projection screen.

She becomes:

- The **Mother** he never reconciled with.

- The **Lover** who reflects his unmet longing.

- The **Temptress** who evokes his guilt around desire.

- The **Mystic** whose depth threatens his control.

- The **Destroyer** who triggers his fear of annihilation.

She becomes **too much**—and therefore, *the problem*.

But in truth, she is only revealing **how little he knows himself.**

The Masculine's Inherited Split

For thousands of years, patriarchal structures have conditioned men to separate themselves from the Feminine—both externally in relationship and internally within the psyche.

This split has left many men unable to recognize the Feminine as sacred. Instead, she becomes unpredictable, seductive, dangerous, unstable—everything he does not yet know how to **hold** within himself.

When a man is disconnected from his own inner Feminine—his receptivity, intuition, emotion, mystery—he will fear these qualities in women. And rather than taking responsibility for that fear, he will label her as the threat.

This is not because she is dangerous.
It is because he is **unfamiliar with his own depth**.

How Projection Becomes Pattern

These projections are not isolated. They become relational patterns.

- The man who unconsciously projects his inner chaos onto the Feminine will seek control, emotionally withdraw, or idealize and then resent her.

- The man who idolizes her to avoid seeing himself will eventually feel betrayed—not by her, but by the fantasy he created.

- The man who represses his own wildness will be threatened by hers and will try to tame, diminish, or shame it.

This cycle repeats until one thing happens:
He turns inward.

Until then, he will continue to ask her to carry the weight of what he refuses to meet inside himself.

From Projection to Integration

The journey out of projection begins not with fixing the relationship, but with facing the reflection.

When a man meets a woman who triggers his deepest emotions—who evokes confusion, rage, infatuation, despair—it is not a sign that she is wrong. It is a sign that his **psyche is being invited into the next initiation**.

She is not the enemy. She is the key.

This doesn't mean every woman is safe. Nor does it mean boundaries are unnecessary.
But it means the man must first ask:

> "What am I seeing in her that lives, unacknowledged, within me?"

This is not surrendering to her.
It is **returning to himself**.

Embodiment Practice: Reclaiming the Projection

Exercise: The Inner Mirror

- Sit in stillness. Recall a moment when a woman triggered something intense in you—anger, desire, fear, longing.

- Hold her image in your mind.

- Now ask: *What quality in her am I resisting, fearing, or idealizing?*

- Find that same quality in yourself.

    - Where is it alive?

    - Where have you buried it?

    - What would it feel like to reclaim it?

Breathe into that reclaimed trait. Speak aloud:

> *"I take back what I projected. I welcome this part of me home."*

Reflection Ritual: Journal Inquiry

1. What qualities in women consistently trigger strong emotional reactions in me?

2. How might these be reflections of disowned parts of myself?

3. Where do I fear or reject the Feminine—both in others and within me?

4. What would integration of my inner Feminine look and feel like?

Integration Oracle: The Feminine Responds

"I was never too much. I was the part of you waiting to be remembered."
"I never wanted to break you. I wanted to show you your own depth."
"I do not need your control. I need your presence."

The projection is not the problem.
The refusal to meet it is.

The Feminine is not the distortion.
She is the **invitation**.

To see what is broken.
To feel what is buried.
To reclaim what was yours all along.

Chapter 2, Subsection 6: THE RAGE BENEATH THE SILENCE
(Mythopoetic Narrative – Balanced Prose – Expanded)

Invocation: The Fire That Had No Voice

There is a fire that lives beneath the surface of many men.
It does not announce itself loudly.
It flickers behind the eyes, clenches in the jaw, tightens in the chest.
It shows up in quiet withdrawal, in cutting sarcasm, in explosive moments that feel out of proportion.

Most men don't even know it's there—
until it leaks.

This is not just anger.
It is **rage**.
Ancient.
Inherited.
Suppressed for generations.

It is the voice that was never allowed to speak.
The boy who was told to sit still.
The man who gave everything and was told it wasn't enough.

This rage is not wrong.
It is the part of him that remembers he was never meant to be this silent.

Where Rage Begins

Rage is the aftershock of abandonment.
It is not born in chaos, but in silence.
It grows in the gap between a man's truth and his reality.

When a boy is told:

- "Don't cry."

- "Be strong."

- "That didn't hurt."

- "You're being dramatic."

He learns to mistrust his inner world. He is taught to regulate not through awareness, but through suppression. Over time, what isn't expressed doesn't disappear—it mutates.

Grief becomes resentment.
Pain becomes withdrawal.
Powerlessness becomes rage.

Not the sacred kind.
But the volatile, unconscious kind—
the kind that surfaces when the body can no longer carry what the mind refused to name.

The Difference Between Anger and Rage

Anger is clean.
It is directional, precise, grounded in present-time truth.
It sets boundaries. It defends the sacred.

Rage, however, is historical.
It is the accumulation of a thousand moments of suppression.
It is anger that was denied a voice so many times that it now speaks with a roar.

Men carrying rage often don't know how to access it in its clean form.
So they:

- Numb it.

- Spiritualize it.

- Leak it in passive-aggression or domination.

- Turn it inward as depression, illness, or apathy.

Rage isn't the enemy.
It's the **signal**.
It tells us where life was dishonored.

The Shame Around Male Rage

Our culture fears male rage—and with good reason.
We have seen it destroy.
We have seen it turn into abuse, violence, and generational trauma.

But because we fear what rage becomes when repressed and weaponized, we often never give men space to work with it consciously. Instead, we shame them out of it.

The result?
 More repression.
 More explosions.
 More isolation.

We do not heal male rage by condemning it.
 We heal it by **listening to what it's trying to protect.**

What Rage Protects

Underneath every man's rage is a younger self.
 One who was:

- Unheard.

- Disrespected.

- Violated.

- Silenced.

- Unprotected.

Rage is the body's demand that we finally turn toward that boy.
 That we acknowledge he was wronged.
 That we stop asking him to carry the silence of his fathers.

When a man listens to his rage without fusing with it,
 he can begin the descent into grief, sovereignty, and clarity.

This is the work:
To transform the fire that once destroyed into a flame that protects.

The Sacred Use of Anger

Anger, when integrated, becomes a sword of clarity.
It helps a man say:

- "No more."
- "That ends with me."
- "I deserve to be respected."
- "I will protect what matters."

This is not domination.
This is **guardianship**.

The sacred masculine does not suppress fire.
It learns to hold it, direct it, and use it to **light the way**.

Embodiment Practice: Meeting the Fire

Exercise: The Contained Flame

- Stand tall. Feet shoulder-width apart.
- Place one hand on your lower belly, one on your heart.

- Breathe. Deeply.

- Bring to mind something in your life that evokes anger. Not rage—just clean anger.

- Feel the energy rise. Don't suppress it. Don't act it out. Just breathe into it.

Speak aloud:

> "I am allowed to feel anger."
> "My fire is sacred."
> "I will not use it to harm. I will use it to see."

Let your voice be steady.
Let your body feel strong and soft at once.

Reflection Ritual: Journal Inquiry

1. What messages did I receive about anger growing up?

2. How have I seen rage play out in my life—mine or my lineage's?

3. Where am I afraid of my own fire?

4. What might change if I trusted anger as a guide, not a threat?

Integration Oracle: The Fire Speaks

"I burned because I was ignored."
"I erupted because I was silenced."
"But now that you see me, I no longer need to destroy. I can protect."

You were never wrong for feeling rage.
You were only ever taught to hide it.

Now is the time to bring your fire home.
Not to punish.
But to purify.
To protect what is sacred—starting with you.

THE CORE WOUND OF POWERLESSNESS

Invocation: The King Without a Sword

There is a moment in every man's life when he realizes he cannot protect what he loves.

Not because he lacks strength,
But because something inside him has been severed—
from voice, from clarity, from his center.

It's not always dramatic.
Sometimes, it arrives quietly:
A failure.
A betrayal.
A word he couldn't say.
A child he couldn't save.
A dream he gave up on before it could take root.

And in that moment, whether he knows it or not,
the wound of powerlessness opens.

The First Break in Sovereignty

Powerlessness is not simply the absence of control.
It is the **absence of internal trust**.

It begins early.

- When the boy is punished for speaking truth.

- When he's told his emotions are irrational.
- When he cries for help, and no one comes.
- When his attempts to act with integrity are mocked or ignored.

Each time, a subtle fracture forms in the psyche.
He learns that his **inner compass cannot be trusted**.
That truth is dangerous.
That action is either futile or punished.

So he stops reaching.
He stops leading.
And eventually—he stops believing he has the right to choose at all.

How Powerlessness Becomes the Core Wound

The wound deepens over time.
Not because it is inherently strong,
But because it is rarely named.

It becomes internalized as a silent belief:

> *"I am not enough."*
> *"Nothing I do matters."*
> *"No one will listen."*
> *"I can't change anything."*

This belief slowly rots the roots of sovereignty.
A man might still appear strong, even successful.

But beneath the surface, he is operating from a place of subtle collapse.

He may become passive in relationships, unsure in purpose, or obsessive about control.
He may bounce between apathy and performance, shame and aggression.

Because somewhere within,
he feels like a king without a sword—
a man who was born to lead, but never taught how.

The Disempowered Masculine Archetypes

When powerlessness is not healed, it mutates into shadow forms:

- The **Passive Prince** – waits to be chosen, avoids responsibility.

- The **Shadow King** – dominates to mask his inner doubt.

- The **Wounded Warrior** – fights battles he doesn't believe he can win.

- The **Ghost Father** – present in form, absent in energy.

- The **Saboteur** – destroys what's good before it can leave him.

Each of these archetypes is a **compensation strategy**, an attempt to survive life with a broken inner compass.

But none of them lead to wholeness.
They only deepen the silence.

Reclaiming Power from Within

Powerlessness is healed not by seizing control—
but by **remembering that your voice, your presence, and your choices matter.**

This is not about reclaiming the illusion of dominance.
It is about reclaiming **agency**, **responsibility**, and **right-sized power**.

You are not here to control life.
You are here to **meet it fully.**

Power is not about force.
Power is the ability to stay connected to truth—
even when the world feels unstable.

This is the root of mature masculinity:
inner leadership before outer control.

The Moment of Choice

Every man must one day stand at this threshold:

- Will I live as the one who waits to be chosen...
  or will I choose myself?

- Will I continue performing power, or will I **embody it from within**?

- Will I keep blaming others for my stagnation, or will I claim my role in the story I'm writing?

This is not a moment of grand triumph.
It's usually a quiet decision.
A breath.
A truth spoken.
A step taken.

It doesn't feel like fireworks.
It feels like coming home.

Embodiment Practice: The Reclamation of Choice

Exercise: I Choose

- Stand upright. Close your eyes.

- Bring to mind a place in your life where you feel stuck or helpless.

- Feel the energy of that stuckness in your body—let it be present.

Now breathe into your spine. Feel the vertical line of your being.
Speak aloud:

"I am not helpless. I am choosing now."
"I release the belief that I must wait for permission."
"I reclaim my power—not as force, but as presence."

Take one step forward.
Make it real.

Reflection Ritual: Journal Inquiry

1. What is one early memory where I felt powerless—and internalized that feeling?

2. Where in my life do I still act as if I have no real choice?

3. What beliefs have I inherited about power, action, or voice?

4. What does true, embodied, mature power feel like to me?

Integration Oracle: The Inner King Speaks

"You were never powerless. You were only disconnected."
"You do not need the world's permission to act from truth."
"Power is not control—it is coherence between soul and action."

There is a sword buried in the soil of your own becoming.
It will not be handed to you.
But it will rise when you choose to stop abandoning yourself.

You were never meant to live small.
You were meant to **stand, speak, and stay**.

This is where sovereignty begins.

Chapter 3: THE CULTURE OF PERFORMANCE

This is where the act ends.

You've performed long enough.
The charm. The strength. The self-sufficiency.
All of it held together by a thread of fear:
"If I drop the act, will anyone stay?"

This is the dismantling of the false masculine contract.
This is where performance gives way to presence.

It will feel like loss.
It will feel like freedom.
Sometimes, both in the same breath.

This chapter is your quiet revolt.
Your silent unmasking.
Your return.

Threshold Invocation: The Stage Beneath the Skin

Before you move forward, pause.
Ask yourself: Who taught you that being seen was more important than being real?
Who taught you that the right mask was worth more than the wrong truth?

This is your next threshold.

Beyond it lies the **Second Veil**—the architecture of a performance so convincing that even you began to believe it.
This isn't the performance of theater. It's the **performance of identity**.
The role you didn't choose, but rehearsed for years.

Step in.
Not as an actor.
But as the one who finally breaks the fourth wall.

The Masculine on Stage

The modern man has not just been told *how* to behave.
He has been **trained** to perform a version of manhood so refined, so reward-based, so socially sanctioned,
that he often doesn't realize it's a role at all.

From a young age, boys are handed scripts:

- Be strong, not soft.
- Be competent, not curious.
- Be composed, not chaotic.
- Be admired, not authentic.

And so begins the performance.
He learns the lines.
He hits his marks.
He earns applause in the form of money, status, sex, or approval.
And yet—deep beneath the applause,
he feels **nothing**.

Because it isn't his life.
It's a play he was cast in without consent.

Symbolic Collapse Checkpoint #1: The Identity Shell

You are not your job.
You are not your confidence.
You are not your productivity.
You are not the image in her eyes or theirs.
You are not the performance.

This identity construct—the Self you think you must uphold—
is a **protective shell**,
but it is not your soul.

And it cannot hold the weight of your truth.

It is **too brittle**.
It was never meant to be real.
Only to be approved.

And now, the shell is cracking.

The Reward System of the False Masculine

The culture of performance is reinforced by reward systems that feed the ego but starve the essence.

- You show strength? You are celebrated.
- You show pain? You are pitied or dismissed.
- You succeed? You're a man.
- You fail? You're questioned.
- You win? You're worthy.
- You feel? You're fragile.

Every performance gets applause.
But inside the performer, a part of you begins to whisper:

> "If they love the act, what happens when I drop it?"

And that whisper becomes a tremor.
A question.
A reckoning.

Because at some point, every man who performs long enough begins to wonder if **he has ever been truly seen at all**.

The Crisis Beneath the Success

This is the part few talk about.

Many men reach their goals.
They get the house, the title, the woman, the wealth.
And yet they sit in silence at night
wondering why they still feel hollow.

This is not depression.
It's **disorientation**.
A kind of soul vertigo that sets in when your outer life no longer matches your inner truth.

This is when the Second Veil begins to shimmer.
And behind it, something deeper calls.

> *"Drop the act. Let the audience go. Come back to the truth."*

Symbolic Collapse Checkpoint #2: The False Role Unwritten

Let this land.

You do not need to keep performing.
You do not need to keep producing to prove you deserve to exist.

You are not your metrics.
You are not your mask.

You are the one who remembers—
when the lights go down,
when the stage is empty,
when you breathe again and realize
you were never meant to be a character.

You are the author.
You are the origin.
You are the flame.

Dimensional Reorientation: Fractal Identity Reclaiming

At this point in the journey, time begins to bend.

You are remembering not only your own life—
but all the lives you were told to live instead.
You begin to see the loops, the recursions:

- Every achievement that left you emptier.

- Every compliment that deepened the mask.

- Every relationship where you played the role of "man" instead of being human.

This is not regression.
It is **reconvergence**.

All those false paths begin folding back into the now.
And now, you choose.

Embodiment Practice: Dropping the Role

Exercise: Mirror of Unmasking

- Stand before a mirror. Let yourself soften.
- Look into your own eyes.
- Ask: *"What part of me have I hidden to be loved?"*
- Breathe into the answer. Don't flinch.

Then say aloud:

> *"I release the need to perform. I remember who I am beneath the applause."*
> *"I do not exist for others' expectations. I exist for truth."*

Let the body drop its tension.
Let the face return to stillness.
Let the act end.

Reflection Ritual: Journal Inquiry

1. Where in my life do I feel the pressure to perform rather than simply be?
2. What part of my identity is most tied to external approval?

3. What would I feel if I stopped performing for just one day?

4. Who am I when no one is watching?

Integration Oracle: The Curtain Falls

"The world does not need more perfect men. It needs present men."
"You were not born to perform. You were born to embody."
"The act is over. The truth begins now."

Step off the stage.
Walk into the dark unknown.
Let the silence wrap around you like truth.

Your power is not in how you are seen.
It is in how you **stand without needing to be seen at all.**

This is the threshold.

You are no longer the mask.
You are the mirror.
You are the man.

IDENTITY AND IMAGE ADDICTION

Threshold Invocation: The Temple of Reflections

You are now entering the hall of mirrors.
Not the mirrors that reflect your face—
But the ones that reflect the **identity constructs you've mistaken for truth.**

Look carefully.

Every reflection here is built from survival.
Some from shame.
Some from longing.
Some from pride.

Each one whispers,

> "This is who you must be to be enough."

This is the trap.
The addiction to image.
The fractal distortion of identity.

And it is the next veil you must pass through,
if you are to ever remember who you truly are.

The Fracturing of the Self

In a world obsessed with optics, image becomes more important than integrity.
And so men begin to **fracture**.

Not externally—
but **internally**, into personas.

The Provider.
The Protector.
The Performer.
The Rebel.
The Stoic.
The Saint.

Each role is designed to evoke validation.
To protect against rejection.
To ensure the man is seen as "valuable."

But beneath it all…
the core Self begins to fade.

Not because it is weak,
but because it was never invited to the surface.

Symbolic Collapse Checkpoint #3: Image as Cage

Let this truth burn through:

Your image—crafted so carefully to be impressive, desirable, or strong—

is not your essence.
It is a cage built from mirrors.

Every time you update your reflection to match others' expectations,
you reinforce the illusion that you must **earn your identity**.

But identity is not earned.
It is **reclaimed**.

And no one else can give it to you.
Especially not the screen.
Especially not the system.
Especially not the past.

The Addiction Loop

Here's how it works:

- You feel the internal void.

- You reach for external confirmation to fill it.

- You get approval, attention, praise.

- It soothes you—for a moment.

- Then it fades.

- The void returns.

- You reach again.

This is image addiction.

It is subtle.
 Socially rewarded.
 Deadly to the soul.

Because every time you source your worth from how you appear,
 you feed the **phantom self**—
 and starve the real one.

The False Reflection Principle

You've been looking in the wrong mirror.
 Not the one in your home—
 but the one you carry inside.

The mirror of comparison.
 Of social metrics.
 Of past projections.
 Of your father's unmet expectations.
 Of her disappointment.
 Of your younger self's fantasy of who you "should" be by now.

This mirror doesn't reflect truth.
 It reflects distortion.

To break free, you must stop asking your reflection for permission to be real.

The Grief of Letting Go of Who You Pretended to Be

There is pain here.
 And it must be honored.

Letting go of the image you've spent years curating isn't just a shift—
It's a kind of **death**.

You mourn the version of yourself you *wanted* to be,
the one you hoped would finally feel worthy.

And in that mourning, something beautiful happens:

The performance dies.
The person returns.

This grief is not your enemy.
It is your rite of passage.

Dimensional Awareness: Identity Is a Temporary Tool, Not a Self

The most sacred teachings of ancient initiatory paths all point to this:

You are not your identity.
Identity is a necessary tool—
but when confused for the Self, it becomes a prison.

In quantum space, identity is **fluid**, **non-local**, **ever-shifting**.

In sacred space, it is **optional**.

You are not meant to cling to a single version of yourself—
You are meant to **remember the One beneath all roles.**

This is your essence.
Unnameable.

Unshakable.
Unseen by the eye,
but undeniable to the soul.

Embodiment Practice: The Mirror Ritual

Exercise: Break the Reflection

- Sit in a dimly lit room with a mirror before you.

- Bring to mind the identity you've performed most often—The Achiever? The Stoic? The Savior?

- Let your face take on that persona. Observe yourself. Feel the tension it creates.

Now close your eyes.
Breathe deeply.
Release the image. Let your face soften.
Then open your eyes again and whisper:

> "I release this mask. I no longer serve the mirror. I remember the man beneath."

Stay with your own gaze for one minute.
No image. Just essence.

Reflection Ritual: Journal Inquiry

1. What identity do I most rely on for approval?

2. What emotions arise when I imagine letting that identity go?

3. Where do I perform instead of relate?

4. Who am I becoming when I stop trying to be anyone at all?

Integration Oracle: The Mirror Shatters

"You do not need to be impressive. You need to be present."
"You are not a reflection. You are the light."
"Let them forget who you were—so you can remember who you are."

Let the old image collapse.

Let the real one rise—slowly, subtly, powerfully.
Not to be seen.
But to be felt.
To be known.
To be **lived.**

You are no longer an image.
You are a presence.
You are the real.

THE SUBCONSCIOUS MASCULINE PERFORMANCE LOOP

Threshold Invocation: The Loop Within the Labyrinth

Welcome to the hidden layer. The one behind the curtain of your own awareness.
You've broken the first mirrors.
You've begun shedding the identity-skins stitched from expectation.
But now you enter a subtler terrain—
the domain not of image,
but of **automation**.

This is the loop.

Not just a behavior.
Not just a belief.
But a **subconscious architecture**—
a self-reinforcing pattern encoded into the masculine psyche over generations.

You didn't choose this.
But it *is* yours now.
And unless you decode it,
it will continue to live **your life for you**.

Understanding the Loop: What It Is, and Why It Exists

The **Subconscious Masculine Performance Loop** is a psycho-emotional algorithm formed through **cultural encoding**, **generational trauma**, and **early psychological imprinting**.

It has three core components:

1. Internalized Masculine Programming

This is the inherited script:

- "My worth comes from what I do."
- "I must perform to belong."
- "I must succeed to be respected."
- "My emotions are dangerous."
- "My softness is a liability."

These beliefs are rarely questioned—because they are absorbed before the age of conscious discernment.

2. Compensatory Behavior Loops

This is how the psyche survives the original wound of disconnection.

> I feel unworthy → I perform.
> I perform → I receive approval.
> Approval feels like love → I perform more.
> But I still feel hollow → I push harder.

Round and round.

A man may live decades inside this spiral without realizing he's in it.

3. Subconscious Identity Reinforcement

Because performance becomes the means of receiving love and safety, the subconscious begins to **build a Self around the act**.

This is not true identity.
It's a protective avatar.

It looks like confidence.
It sounds like certainty.
But it's **driven by a fear of being truly seen.**

Symbolic Collapse Checkpoint #4: The Loop Is Not You

Pause here.

Feel the truth of this:

> The performance loop is not your fault.
> But it is no longer your path.

You are not your conditioning.
You are not your compulsion.
You are not the loop.

You are the one who *can witness it now*.
And that witnessing is the first crack in the algorithm.

The Origins of the Loop: Generational and Archetypal

This loop didn't begin with you.

It is a system passed from father to son, teacher to student, society to soul.

- When the father was emotionally absent, the son learned to overperform to feel seen.

- When failure was punished, the child internalized perfectionism as survival.

- When anger was dangerous, the man became numb.

- When depth was mocked, the boy learned to stay shallow.

And the lineage continues…
 until someone sees the loop, names it, and **chooses a different path**.

That someone is you.

How the Loop Feeds on Itself

Here's the genius—and the tragedy—of the loop:

It's self-reinforcing.
 Because the more you perform, the more approval you get.

And the more approval you get, the harder it becomes to risk authenticity.

Eventually, the loop *feels like identity*.

But here's the signal that something is off:

No matter how much you succeed,
 how much you give,
 how perfect you become—
 it's never enough.

That's not because you're broken.
 It's because **you're living inside a pattern that was never built to lead you home.**

The Exit Point: Pattern Recognition → Pattern Collapse

The loop cannot be "fixed" through willpower.
 It must be **made conscious**.
 Witnessed.
 Felt.
 And grieved.

The moment you begin to notice:

> "Ah, this isn't me. This is the script."
> "This is the loop trying to protect me again."
> "This is my nervous system responding to old coding."

That's when it begins to unravel.

Not overnight.
But organically.
One honest moment at a time.

Dimensional Expansion: Identity as Awareness, Not Algorithm

As you exit the loop, your identity no longer lives in the **doing**. It begins to root in the **being**.

This is the **quantum masculine**—
A man who acts from *conscious choice*, not conditioned reflex.
A man whose presence isn't tied to performance, but to purpose.

This is not passivity.
This is power.
The kind that cannot be threatened,
because it is not based on outcome.
It's based on **presence**.

Embodiment Practice: Interrupting the Loop

Exercise: The Interrupting Breath

- When you feel the familiar compulsion to perform, please, prove, or perfect—pause.

- Place a hand on your heart and belly.

- Inhale for 4, hold for 4, exhale for 6.

- Ask:
  "Is this action coming from alignment or old pattern?"
  "Am I choosing this—or am I surviving something I haven't named?"

Breathe again.
Then choose—consciously, gently, truthfully.

Reflection Ritual: Journal Inquiry

1. What recurring pattern in my life feels like a loop I can't escape?

2. When did I first learn that performance equals safety or love?

3. What would my life look like if I no longer had to earn worth through action?

4. How can I begin making conscious choices instead of reflexive performances?

Integration Oracle: The Loop Is Not the Man

"You are not your automation. You are awareness."
"The loop ends not with force, but with presence."
"Every time you choose truth over reflex, you rewire your becoming."

You are not a reaction.
You are a revolution.
One breath, one pause, one act of awareness at a time.

The loop ends here.
And something ancient begins to awaken—
not the man you were trained to be,
but the one you came here to become.

THE COLLAPSE OF FALSE CONFIDENCE

Threshold Invocation: The Shattering Smile

This is the moment the man who always seemed sure of himself… stops pretending.

The smile falters.
The posture cracks.
The certainty evaporates.

And what's left?
Not failure.
Not weakness.

But the **truth** that was buried beneath the image of confidence all along.

This is the **Collapse of False Confidence**—not the end of your power,
but the sacred destruction of the version of you that never had access to it.

You are not losing yourself.
You are losing the mask.

The Performance of Confidence

False confidence is subtle.

It doesn't always look loud or arrogant.
Sometimes, it looks like:

- Always having an answer.

- Avoiding vulnerability by appearing composed.

- Speaking from certainty when the soul is still unsure.

- Holding it together at all costs—especially when falling apart would be honest.

- Never letting anyone see your confusion.

This kind of confidence is constructed—
layered over time, woven into your nervous system.
It was **never real**—but it was necessary.

It kept you safe.
It bought you belonging.
It helped you survive.

But it will not help you become.

Symbolic Collapse Checkpoint #5: The Myth of Certainty

Let go of this myth now:

> "A man must always know."
> "A man must always lead."
> "A man must never show doubt."

These were never truths.
They were **defenses against exposure**.

In truth, false confidence is not power.
It's a bypass.

A bypass of:

- Fear.

- Tenderness.

- Unknowing.

- Surrender.

Real power begins when a man can stand in his uncertainty and still stay present.
Still stay open.
Still stay *real*.

The Collapse: When the Persona Fails

There comes a moment—often sudden, often unplanned—when the mask slips.

- The relationship ends, and charm no longer protects you.

- The business collapses, and no performance can hold it together.

- The words dry up, and you're left with silence.

- The anger comes, and it breaks through the smile.

It feels like failure.
It feels like freefall.

But what's happening is this:

Your soul is refusing to be hidden any longer.

What Emerges in the Collapse

Once the performance falls, what remains is not ruin.
It's rawness.
It's truth.

It's the boy who never learned how to be seen without performing.
It's the man who realizes he has never spoken from the center of his being.

This is not a breakdown.
This is a **clearing**.

Your voice may shake.
Your face may flush.
Your certainty may vanish.

Good.

Now, finally, you are becoming trustworthy.

Confidence vs. Coherence

Confidence that comes from the mind can be powerful, but it is easily shaken.

Confidence that comes from the ego is reactive and performative.

But **coherence**—the alignment of body, truth, voice, and soul—cannot be faked.

It is quiet.
It is magnetic.
It does not need to prove itself.

This is where you're going now.

Not toward confidence,
but toward **energetic congruence**.

Where what you say, what you feel, what you choose, and what you are—
are finally one.

Fractal Collapse and Archetypal Rebirth

In myth, the false self must die before the real self can emerge.

- The warrior must fall to find his soul.

- The king must be dethroned to become sovereign.

- The sage must forget everything to truly know.

This is that moment.

The false confidence must collapse
so the **true root of your power can rise**.

This is not just personal.
It is archetypal.

You are standing in the ashes of your former image.
Do not rebuild it.
Let something deeper emerge.

Embodiment Practice: The Ground of Unknowing

Exercise: Sitting in the Unknown

- Sit in stillness. Close your eyes.

- Name one area of life where you feel you must appear confident.

- Let that pressure go. Drop into the sensation of not knowing.

- Breathe into the space it creates.

- Say aloud:

    "I allow myself to not know."
    "I release the performance of power."
    "What rises in me now will be real."

Sit longer than is comfortable.
Let the silence become familiar.

Reflection Ritual: Journal Inquiry

1. Where have I performed confidence instead of embodying truth?

2. What fear is beneath my need to appear sure?

3. What would it feel like to be coherent, not just confident?

4. What does my real power feel like in the absence of performance?

Integration Oracle: The Real Voice Emerges

"When you stopped performing, the world began to hear you."
"When you stopped pretending, your body finally exhaled."
"You do not need to be sure. You only need to be here."

Let false confidence fall.

What rises now will not be hollow.
It will not be rehearsed.
It will be yours.

Real.
Rooted.
Ready.

INITIATION THROUGH HUMILIATION

Threshold Invocation: The Fall Before the Flame

This is the part no one talks about.
The part where the image shatters,
the voice breaks,
the pride buckles beneath its own weight.

Not because you're weak—
but because your soul is about to take the reins.

This is the *initiation through humiliation*,
the sacred fall that feels like failure,
but is actually a rite of **ego disarmament**.

You are not being punished.
You are being purified.

What Humiliation Really Is

In our culture, humiliation is seen as shameful.
Embarrassment. Exposure. A fall from grace.

But in truth, **humiliation is the collapse of a false hierarchy within the self.**

It is the sacred process by which the **mask gets cracked**,
and the *truth begins to breathe.*

When a man is humiliated,
it is not his worth being destroyed—
it is his illusion being dismantled.

> It is the unraveling of the persona
> that was never built to carry his soul.

The Archetypal Pattern: The Shattering of the False King

Every authentic hero journey requires a descent.
The warrior must lose.
The king must fall.
The sage must forget.
The father must face his own fragility.

It is in the *humbling* that the real power begins to rise.

This is when the false king is dethroned—
the one who ruled through fear, control, performance, or pride.

And in his place, the **sovereign self** begins to stir.

Not louder.
But deeper.
Not more confident.
More coherent.

Humiliation as Initiation, Not Defeat

To be humiliated is to be:

- Stripped.
- Witnessed.
- Unmasked.
- Flattened.

And in that flattening,
 something ancient awakens.

> A man who has nothing left to prove
> becomes the most trustworthy man in the room.

He speaks slower.
 Listens deeper.
 Moves from his center, not from performance.

The humiliation becomes an altar,
 and the broken pride becomes **kindling for the new flame**.

The Lineage of Sacred Falling

Across spiritual and mythic traditions, the **collapse precedes the crown**.

- Christ before resurrection.
- Odin on the tree.
- Arjuna before the battle.
- The monk in exile.

- The father who weeps when his child sees his brokenness—and loves him anyway.

In each story, the *fall* is the turning point.
Not the failure.

You are not being brought low to be crushed.
You are being **unmade so you can be made true**.

What Happens After the Fall

After the humiliation, there is quiet.

A man who has wept in front of his child,
 failed in front of his tribe,
 been left, broken, forgotten—

And yet who stays with himself
 doesn't come back the same.

His movements are simpler.
 His voice—more precise.
 His words—fewer, but heavier.
 His eyes—more honest.

This is the **initiation through collapse**.
The **grace of being stripped clean**.

Symbolic Collapse Checkpoint #6: You Are Still Worthy

Let this truth ring through your nervous system:

> "I am still worthy in my fall."
> "I am still loved in my breaking."
> "I am still a man in my weeping."

In fact, this is often the first moment
you *finally* become one.

Not because others say so—
but because the mirror no longer lies.

You have stopped running.
And now you can begin again.

Embodiment Practice: Ritual of the Fall

Exercise: The Grounding of the Broken

- Sit on the floor. Let your spine curve, your head hang.

- Feel the weight of every mask you've held—let it drop.

- Whisper to yourself:

  > "I don't know who I am without the performance. And that's okay."
  > "I am still breathing. I am still here. I am still worthy."

Now slowly rise, vertebra by vertebra.
Do not rush.
Let it be **a resurrection, not a recovery**.

Stand tall.
But not like before.
This time, you are rooted.

Reflection Ritual: Journal Inquiry

1. When was the last time I felt humiliated? What was actually being stripped away?

2. How have I equated shame with worthlessness?

3. What version of myself was dismantled in that moment—and what truth emerged?

4. Can I allow myself to be seen in my fall, and still claim my space?

Integration Oracle: The Initiate Speaks

"What you lost was not you. It was what you built to be loved."
"Let it fall. Let it crack. Let it burn."
"Your sovereignty begins in the place you once thought you'd never rise from."

The fall is holy.
The collapse is sacred.

And you, brother, are not broken.
 You are becoming.

THE REBIRTH OF THE AUTHENTIC SELF

Threshold Invocation: The Return to the Flame

You've fallen.
Not into failure—
but into **truth**.

The roles have cracked.
The mask has melted.
The illusion has burned.

And now, you rise.

Not as a man reborn into perfection,
but as a man finally **reunited with what was always true**.

Welcome to the **Rebirth of the Authentic Self**.

This is not the end of your undoing.
It is the beginning of your *embodiment*.

What Is the Authentic Self?

It's not a personality.
Not a performance.
Not a polished identity that impresses.

The authentic self is **the core essence** of who you are when nothing is left to protect, prove, or perform.

It's the version of you that:

- Breathes without bracing.
- Speaks without seeking approval.
- Loves without bargaining.
- Stands without armor.

This Self has always been within you—
but buried beneath decades of adaptation, survival, and silence.

Now, after the fall,
you are free to return to it.

Archetypal Resurrection: From Fragmentation to Wholeness

In the sacred rites of every mythic path,
there is a point beyond collapse—
a moment when the man who has been dismantled
remembers who he truly is.

He does not remember in the mind.
He remembers in the *body*.
In the breath.
In the ground beneath his feet.

And it is here, in this simple presence,
that he becomes *whole* again.

Not perfect.
  True.

Not flawless.
  Integrated.

Not above others.
  But *rooted in himself*, finally.

The Self You Could Not Access Until Now

There are parts of you
  that only reveal themselves **after surrender.**

Why?

Because the Authentic Self is not reached through effort.
  It is accessed through **allowance.**

It waits.
  Not to be achieved.
  But to be *remembered.*

And now, you are ready.

You've walked through the fire.
  You've seen your shadows.
  You've collapsed the masks.

And in the ash, you find something sacred:
  your undivided essence.

What the Authentic Self Feels Like

It's not loud.
It doesn't need to be.

It feels like:

- Grounded breath.
- Honest words.
- Nervous system coherence.
- Saying "no" without guilt.
- Saying "yes" without performance.
- Leading from alignment, not obligation.
- Loving with open palms, not clenched fists.

It's not about getting it right.
It's about **not abandoning yourself** when things go wrong.

Symbolic Resurrection Checkpoint #7: This Is You Now

Repeat this slowly, with breath:

> "I am not who I was told to be."
> "I am not who I pretended to be."
> "I am the man who remembers who he is—beneath it all."

Let that settle.
This is not affirmation.
This is **activation**.

You're not trying to believe it.
You're choosing to **embody** it.

The world will feel different now.
Because you're no longer navigating it through distortion.

Fractal Integration: Returning Without Regressing

This rebirth is not a return to boyhood, or a rejection of what you've learned.

It is a **sacred integration**.

Now:

- Your power is real.

- Your boundaries are clean.

- Your heart is open, but discerning.

- Your fire is no longer wild—but it still burns.

- Your truth no longer trembles—but it still listens.

You are a man.
Not because someone told you.
Because you chose to become one—from the inside out.

This is the return.
This is the rise.
This is the rebirth.

Embodiment Practice: Sovereign Breathwork

Exercise: Reclaiming the Body of the True Self

- Sit with a tall spine. Hands over heart and belly.

- Inhale for 4. Hold for 4. Exhale for 8. Repeat for five cycles.

- With each breath, whisper:

    "I am here."
    "I am whole."
    "I am the man beneath the mask."

Feel the nervous system settle.
Feel the space within widen.

You're no longer waiting to become yourself.
You already are.

Reflection Ritual: Journal Inquiry

1. What does "authenticity" feel like in my body—not just as a concept, but a sensation?

2. Where in my life am I still tempted to perform instead of express?

3. What am I discovering about myself now that I never had access to before?

4. What does my sovereignty look like when no one is watching?

Integration Oracle: The Soul Speaks

"I was always here, waiting behind the masks."
"Now that you've fallen, you can finally stand as you are."
"No one else can live your truth for you."

You are not your past.
You are not your patterns.
You are not your projections.

You are the man who has *seen himself*,
and stayed.

This is not the end of the journey.
This is where it begins to matter.

Welcome back, brother.
You made it through.

Chapter 4: FEAR OF TRUE INTIMACY

The heart won't open through strength. It opens through surrender.

*You are now standing at the most vulnerable gate:
Not the gate of power, but of closeness.
The place where love touches the wound.*

*This is not romantic. It is elemental.
Because real intimacy does not arrive gently.
It unmakes. It reflects. It asks everything.*

If you let it, this chapter will undo the last layer of armor you thought you still needed.

*You don't need to be ready.
You only need to stay.*

Threshold Invocation: The Gaze That Doesn't Look Away

You've taken off the armor.
You've stood in the fire.
You've collapsed into truth and risen from ash.

But now comes the most disorienting threshold of all:
Letting someone else see you—before you've perfected what they'll see.

This is the Third Veil:
The Fear of True Intimacy.

Not sex. Not connection.
Not affection, attention, or attachment.

Intimacy.
As in: *"into-me-you-see."*

The question is:
Can you allow it?

What Intimacy Actually Is

True intimacy is not proximity.
It's not about touch.
It's not even about love.

It is the **sacred capacity to be seen in your unguarded state—without defense or disguise**.

It means:

- Speaking what you feel before you've made it sound wise.

- Letting your silence be heard.

- Letting your longing be visible.

- Staying when the instinct is to disappear.

- Receiving without needing to earn.

Intimacy is the death of the last mask:
The idea that *you must become something in order to be loved.*

The Origin of the Fear

This fear is primal.
It is not irrational.
It is rooted in memory—personal, ancestral, collective.

Because for many men, being emotionally seen has historically meant:

- Being shamed.

- Being punished.

- Being emasculated.

- Being abandoned.

- Being used.

- Being misunderstood.

So they adapted.
 They learned how to **perform closeness without actually being vulnerable**.

They became experts in:

- Strategic vulnerability.

- Controlled openness.

- Safe disclosure.

And in doing so, they avoided the one thing true intimacy requires:
 Surrender.

Symbolic Collapse Checkpoint #8: She's Not the Threat

Let this settle.

> "It's not the Feminine you're afraid of.
> It's what she might awaken in you."

Because she sees the parts of you that you've spent your whole life managing.

- The part that wants to be held.

- The part that feels small.
- The part that feels too much.
- The part that doubts his own worth.

She doesn't want to break you.
She wants to **meet you**.

But you cannot meet her through performance.
Only through presence.

And presence requires **vulnerability without a script.**

Why True Intimacy Feels So Dangerous

Because to be seen without your defenses
requires that you trust your own enoughness.

It is the deepest confrontation of all:

"If she sees the real me—will she stay?"

But the real fear is not her leaving.
It's what it will mean if she stays.

Because then, you'll have to receive.
You'll have to believe you are worthy
without performing, achieving, protecting, or proving.

And that...
breaks the old system.

Archetypal Mirror: The Feminine as the Initiator of Full Presence

The Feminine is not your reward.
 She is your **invitation**.

She mirrors not just your light, but your shadows—
 Not to harm you, but to reveal what is unintegrated.

If you recoil from her gaze,
 you are recoiling from your own reflection.

If you collapse beneath her intensity,
 you are collapsing under the weight of your **own unlived truth.**

She does not ask you to be perfect.
 She asks you to be **here.**

And when you stay in that gaze—
 not as the protector, the provider, the performer—
 but as *yourself*,
 you open the doorway to a kind of love
 that no performance could ever earn.

The Risk—and the Reward

True intimacy feels like danger
 because it requires the **death of the self-image you've used to survive.**

But what comes next is worth everything:

- A relationship that doesn't need roles.
- Sex that doesn't require masks.
- Conflict that leads to connection, not collapse.
- Presence that doesn't flinch.
- Love that doesn't retreat at your edges.

This is not softness.
This is **masculine maturity**.

Not the man who hides.
Not the man who conquers.
The man who **lets himself be seen and does not abandon himself when he is.**

Embodiment Practice: The Gaze of Presence

Exercise: Into-Me-You-See

- Sit opposite a trusted partner (or mirror, if alone).
- Breathe into your body. Ground yourself.
- Hold their gaze for 2 minutes without speaking.
- As you do, feel what arises.
- Let your chest soften. Let your face remain open.

Then say aloud (or to your reflection):

> "I am here. Not to impress. Not to protect. Just to be."
> "You are safe to see me. I am safe to be seen."

Hold the gaze.
Let the discomfort pass.
What comes next is **real presence**.

Reflection Ritual: Journal Inquiry

1. When have I equated vulnerability with weakness or danger?

2. What parts of me am I still hiding from those I love most?

3. What does intimacy feel like in my body—what does it threaten, and what might it heal?

4. What would it mean to let myself be loved without performance?

Integration Oracle: The Intimate Self Speaks

"I do not need to be ready. I need to be here."
"I am not too much. I am not too little. I am just real."
"I will not hide the most sacred parts of me in exchange for conditional connection."

Intimacy is the final veil.
 Because it is where love either deepens...
 or disappears.

But you are ready now.
 Not because you've mastered vulnerability—
 but because you're no longer willing to fake connection to avoid it.

Let yourself be seen.

Let yourself stay.

THE ILLUSION OF CONTROL IN LOVE

Threshold Invocation: The Grip That Forgets the Heart

You've stood in the fire.
You've let yourself be seen.
And now, love has begun to feel close—*too* close.
So your hand tightens.
Your rules sharpen.
Your logic rises like a wall.

Because somewhere inside,
you were taught that **to love is to lose control**.

This is the next veil.
The one you thought was strength,
but was really just survival.

Welcome to **The Illusion of Control in Love**.

This isn't about dominance.
This is about the subtle, sacred moment when the Masculine remembers:

> *You cannot protect yourself from love without*
> *also preventing it from reaching you.*

Why We Try to Control Love

The masculine psyche is often raised in systems where unpredictability equals danger.

And love?
Love is nothing *if not unpredictable.*

It is:

- Chaotic.
- Cyclical.
- Emotional.
- Vulnerable.
- Unstructured.
- Impossible to map.

So instead of entering it with openness, many men approach it with tactics:

- Control the emotions.
- Control the timeline.
- Control the story.
- Control her.

- Control yourself.

But control is not love's language.
It is love's **counterfeit**.

Because love only meets you where you are **willing to release the plan**.

The Masculine's Deepest Fear

Underneath control lies a wound that says:

> *"If I surrender here, I will be consumed."*

So the man builds structures.
He becomes strategic.
He intellectualizes.
He detaches—just enough to feel safe.

But this strategy keeps him locked in isolation.

Because love does not want your perfection.
It wants your **presence**.

And presence is something control cannot offer.

Symbolic Collapse Checkpoint #9: Surrender ≠ Weakness

Let this break the old pattern:

> Surrender is not submission.
> It is **sacred receptivity**.
> It is saying, *"I choose to be moved by something greater than my mind."*

In love, this means:

- Feeling without manipulating.

- Listening without fixing.

- Staying without needing to solve.

Control says, *"I'll stay as long as I know what's coming."*
Love says, *"I'll stay even when I don't."*

That is the true test of the Masculine heart:
Can you remain open while the outcome remains unknown?

How Control Shows Up in Relationship

You may not call it control.
You may call it "leadership," "structure," or "clarity."

But the signs are there:

- Needing to know what she feels before you reveal yourself.

- Withholding love until you're sure it's safe.

- Monitoring how much you give to avoid being vulnerable.

- Silently demanding emotional regulation from her so you don't feel overwhelmed.

- Holding the steering wheel so tightly that love stops breathing in the car.

These aren't power.
They are **protective contractions**.

And they keep you from the one thing your heart actually longs for:
A love that is alive, free, and uncontainable.

The False Security of the Fortress

Control promises safety.
But it delivers **loneliness**.

It turns love into a contract, not a covenant.
It turns intimacy into negotiation.
It turns emotional depth into something to be managed.

But no one can fully love you if they are only allowed to love the part of you that's in control.

You must be willing to let someone touch the part of you that *doesn't know what to do next*.

That's not weakness.
That's **devotion**.

Archetypal Reversal: From King of the Castle to Guardian of the Flame

The distorted King builds a fortress and isolates himself inside it.
 He controls everything—but feels nothing.

The Sovereign Guardian builds **a sacred fire**
 and invites love to sit with him in the circle.

He protects not with control,
 but with **clarity**, **presence**, and **willingness to be transformed**.

This is the shift now being asked of you.

Not to hold on tighter—
 but to *let go more consciously*.

To choose love,
 not as possession… but as a path.

Embodiment Practice: Letting Go of the Reins

Exercise: Sacred Breath of Surrender

- Sit in a relaxed posture. Hands open, palms up.

- Inhale deeply, imagining every breath **softening** your grip.

- Exhale slowly, releasing the need to know what's next.

- Say aloud:

    "I release control. I invite truth."
    "I choose presence over performance."
    "I allow love to move me without needing to manage it."

Repeat for five minutes.
Then journal—without editing, guiding, or structuring.

Let love speak through you.

Reflection Ritual: Journal Inquiry

1. Where do I try to control love—consciously or unconsciously?

2. What am I afraid will happen if I let go of the reins?

3. How does control masquerade as leadership in my relationships?

4. What would it feel like to love without managing the outcome?

Integration Oracle: The Voice of Surrender

"You do not lose your power when you let go. You reclaim it from the illusion."
"Let love be wild. Let it burn away the rules."
"You are not here to hold it all. You are here to hold what is real."

When you stop gripping the love,
 you finally feel it.

When you stop managing her,
 you finally meet her.

And when you stop protecting your heart from intimacy,
 you begin to **live inside the fire of devotion**.

This is not loss.
 This is return.

SURRENDER AND THE FEMININE PRINCIPLE

Threshold Invocation: The Opening Beyond Control

You've come far.
You've shattered the illusion of performance.
You've faced the fear of being seen.
You've let love undo your grip.

Now, a deeper invitation arrives—one the masculine often resists most.

Not action.
Not direction.
Not initiation.

Surrender.
Not to a person.
Not to an idea.
But to the *Feminine Principle*—within her, and within you.

To surrender is not to collapse.
It is to open.
To receive.
To *trust the mystery*.

And this...
is where the Masculine remembers how to feel **God again**.

What the Feminine Principle Is

The Feminine is not a gender.
It is not a mood, or a role, or a stereotype.

It is a **cosmic intelligence**.
A living frequency.
A divine archetype of creation, flow, emotion, intuition, and chaos.

She is the river that carves the mountain.
She is the silence between your words.
She is the love you cannot predict, the knowing you cannot explain, the force you cannot control.

She is not here to obey you.
She is here to **invite your deepest self to awaken.**

And if you try to master her, she will disappear.
If you open to her—fully, steadily—she will **breathe life into every part of you you've forgotten.**

What It Means to Surrender to Her

To surrender is not to weaken.
It is to **unclench**.

- To stop trying to hold your partner in place, and instead hold yourself in presence.

- To stop managing the flow, and instead **trust its wisdom**.

- To feel deeply, without immediately trying to fix, frame, or fixate.

- To listen to her waves—*her emotions, her chaos, her beauty*—without needing to cage them in logic.

This is the Masculine in its mature form:
Not reactive.
Not detached.
Not dominating.
But **devoted**.

The Internal Feminine: Meeting Her Within

Most men try to navigate the external Feminine without ever having integrated their **inner Feminine**.

But without inner surrender, outer intimacy becomes unstable.

The inner Feminine is:

- Your ability to feel deeply.

- Your intuition that arrives without proof.

- Your grief that doesn't make sense.

- Your longing that terrifies you.

- Your capacity to receive, to soften, to trust.

She is already in you.
 But if you've never let her speak,
 you'll fear her in every woman who does.

To surrender to the Feminine is to surrender to your own **undomesticated soul**.

Symbolic Collapse Checkpoint #10: The Fear of Being Consumed

Here lies the great masculine myth:

> *"If I surrender to her, I will lose myself."*

But in truth, you do not lose your Self.
 You lose the **false self**.
 The version of you that only exists in control.

And what remains?

- The real King—who rules from presence, not power.
- The real Lover—who can feel without drowning.
- The real Warrior—who protects without armor.
- The real Mystic—who sees beyond sight.

You do not disappear when you surrender.
 You *emerge*.

The Feminine Is the Temple, Not the Test

Many men treat the Feminine like a puzzle to solve.
Or a storm to weather.
Or a danger to manage.

But she is none of these.

She is the **temple** of life.
She is the **womb of remembrance**.
She is the **portal to your unguarded self**.

When you surrender—not in subservience, but in reverence—you become a man who can **meet the mystery without fear**.

And this is the threshold
where love becomes holy.

Embodiment Practice: Surrendered Presence

Exercise: Receiving Her Without Fixing

- With a trusted partner or alone, sit in stillness.

- If with a partner, invite them to speak freely—without filter, without agenda.

- Your task is not to correct, control, or calm.

Only to breathe.
To listen.
To **stay.**

Place one hand on your heart, one on your belly.

Breathe deeply and speak silently:

> *"I am safe to receive."*
> *"I do not need to solve to be present."*
> *"The Feminine is not my enemy. She is my remembering."*

Let her waves move through you, not against you.

Reflection Ritual: Journal Inquiry

1. Where in my life do I still resist the Feminine—emotionally, relationally, spiritually?

2. What does surrender feel like in my body? Where do I tense or grasp instead?

3. How do I relate to my own intuition, emotion, and receptivity?

4. What would it look like to meet the Feminine as a sacred force—not a threat?

Integration Oracle: The Feminine Speaks

"You cannot possess me. You can only be present with me."
"I am not here to test your strength. I am here to invite your truth."
"If you stop bracing, I will show you the depths you were born to hold."

Surrender is not collapse.
Surrender is *access*.

It is the moment you stop guarding against life
and start letting it **move through you**.

This is not about becoming less of a man.
It is about becoming the kind of man
who is no longer afraid to open.

LOVE AS INITIATION

Threshold Invocation: The Flame That Transforms

This is the final veil of the heart.
 Not the fear of love.
 Not the loss of control.
 Not the pain of exposure.

But the realization that **love itself is an initiatory fire—**
 one that does not come to comfort you,
 but to **awaken, unmake, and rebuild you.**

You are not here to fall in love.
 You are here to **become it.**

Not the feeling.
 Not the fantasy.

But the **force** that forges the real from the raw.

This is **Love as Initiation.**
 And it is not gentle.
 It is holy.

Love Is Not the Prize. It Is the Path.

In the old paradigm, love is seen as a destination.

You do the work, heal the wounds, earn the right to receive love.
 As if love is the **reward for becoming perfect.**

But real love doesn't wait until you're ready.
It arrives precisely when you're not.
And it **asks everything of you.**

Love says:

> "You want me?
> Then bring your entire Self.
> The raw, the undone, the trembling, the divine."

Love does not complete you.
It **confronts you**.

It exposes everything within you
that is still afraid to be real.

And in that exposure,
it becomes the **furnace of your transformation**.

The Structure of Love as a Rite

All great initiations have three phases:

1. **Separation** – The self as you knew it must be left behind.

2. **Descent** – The fire of truth reveals what is untrue.

3. **Return** – What emerges is no longer a role, but a soul.

Love follows the same pattern:

- You enter expecting union.

- You discover **disruption**.

- You either resist the transformation, or surrender into rebirth.

Most people run at the second stage.
But those who stay?
They emerge **forged**, not just bonded.
Devoted, not just attached.
Awake, not just in relationship.

Symbolic Collapse Checkpoint #11: Love Is Not Safety

This is the revelation that shatters the fantasy:

> *"Love is not here to protect your ego.*
> *Love is here to **invite your soul forward**."*

When you romanticize love as safety,
you resist the very thing that makes it sacred:
its power to remake you.

The Feminine is not here to make you feel secure.
She is here to bring you face to face
with what you still fear in yourself.

And when you stop defending…
you discover that **your capacity to love is your capacity to stay in truth.**

The Heart as Forge

Your heart is not a fragile organ.
 It is a **forge**.

It was built to hold grief, devotion, longing, joy, rage, surrender, ecstasy—**all at once.**

But only when you stop protecting it
 like a glass relic from childhood.

When you let it burn,
 let it ache,
 let it break,
 let it open again and again—

you discover it is not weak.
 It is **indestructible**.

Not because it never gets hurt—
 but because it knows how to **love through the pain**,
 not around it.

Love as Alchemical Mirror

In love, you will be seen.
 In love, you will be misunderstood.
 In love, you will be adored and confronted in the same breath.

And the question will be:

> *"Will I meet this mirror with presence or projection?"*
> *"Will I armor or anchor?"*
> *"Will I use this fire to hide—or to become?"*

Because love is not something you get.
It is something you **become capable of holding**.

And that capacity expands every time you say:

> *"Even here, I choose truth."*
> *"Even here, I do not run."*

Embodiment Practice: Becoming the Love You Seek

Exercise: Heart as Temple

- Sit in stillness. One hand on your chest, one on your belly.

- Inhale: feel your heart expand.

- Exhale: feel the heat of love as a sacred fire—not sentiment, but power.

- Say aloud:

> *"I no longer seek love as completion. I offer love as a way of being."*
> *"Love is not what I receive. It is who I am, unguarded."*

Let the words echo in the hollows that once held your fear.

Reflection Ritual: Journal Inquiry

1. When have I resisted love's invitation because it asked too much of me?

2. What have I tried to protect myself from in love—and what has that cost me?

3. What does it feel like to let love *change me*, not just soothe me?

4. What becomes possible when I show up not to get love—but to *become* it?

Integration Oracle: Love Speaks

"I am not here to comfort the lie. I am here to awaken the soul."
"You will not lose yourself in me—you will find what you were hiding from."
"If you let me, I will burn away every reason you thought you were unworthy."

Love is not a state.
It is a **summons**.

And if you let it initiate you,
you will emerge not as the man who found the perfect partner—
but as the man who finally stopped hiding from his own heart.

This is not the end of the journey.
It is the ignition of your deepest power.

Love, now, is no longer something you fall into.
It is something you **rise with**.

Chapter 5: THE RETURN OF THE SACRED MASCULINE

You do not earn your crown. You become coherent enough to carry it.

This chapter is not about taking up space.
*It's about **becoming the space**—*
So others can rise beside you.

Leadership is no longer performance.
Power is no longer force.
Purpose is no longer identity.

This is the chapter of rootedness.
Of stewardship.
Of sovereignty.

Walk through this gate, not with noise—
*But with **clear, embodied presence**.*

Threshold Invocation: The Crown Is Remembered, Not Given

You have descended into your shadow.
You have burned through your veils.
You have surrendered your armor, your illusions, your control.

And now...
you are ready to rise.

Not into superiority.
Not into domination.

But into **devotional sovereignty**—
into the **Return of the Sacred Masculine**.

This is not the man who rules.
This is the man who **remembers**.

Not a king above—but a **pillar among**.
Not a warrior seeking battle—but a **guardian of the sacred**.

He does not posture.
He does not perform.

He **becomes**—
by embodying the presence that *cannot be shaken*.

Who the Sacred Masculine Is

The Sacred Masculine is not a concept.
It is a **frequency**.

You know it when you feel it.

It is the man who:

- Moves slowly, because he's not rushing to prove.

- Speaks with silence, because he's no longer afraid of it.

- Holds space, not because he wants control, but because he is deeply attuned.

- Leads, not for power, but from presence.

He is the man whose actions are aligned with spirit.
Whose heart remains open in fire.
Whose truth is clean.
Whose word is bond.

He does not dominate the Feminine.
He **witnesses her, protects her, and learns from her.**

He does not shrink the boy within.
He fathers him, integrates him, and brings him home.

This is not modern masculinity.
This is **primordial remembrance.**

What the Journey Has Forged in You

This return cannot be faked.
 It must be earned—not through performance, but through *willingness to descend.*

And you have.

You've:

- Faced the shame.
- Named the pattern.
- Sat in the ache.
- Stayed in the gaze.
- Let yourself be loved.
- Let yourself be undone.

And now, something older than your name begins to stir.

It is not ego.
 It is not persona.

It is the part of you that **was never broken**.

Symbolic Resurrection Checkpoint #12: You Are Now Becoming the Fire

At every stage, the fire refined you:

- Burned away false power.
- Melted inherited scripts.
- Illuminated hidden grief.
- Tempered your edges.

But now, you are no longer inside the fire.

You are the fire.

Not to destroy.
 But to illuminate.
 To warm.
 To forge.
 To guide.

This is what it means to be sacred.

To become a **source**—not of control, but of coherence.

The Four Pillars of the Sacred Masculine

Let this transmission seed itself in your being:

1. Presence

You are rooted in the moment.
 Unshaken. Unrushed. Unattached to outcome.
 People feel safer just by your existence.

2. Integrity

Your inner and outer align.
What you say becomes law—not because you are perfect,
but because you are accountable.

3. Devotion

You are loyal to what is holy, not what is comfortable.
You serve life, not ego.
You lead through love, not hierarchy.

4. Wisdom

You listen before speaking.
You create before reacting.
You see beneath what others show.
You hold paradox without needing to resolve it.

You do not need to explain this.
You only need to **embody it**.

This Is Not the End—It Is the Beginning

You are not returning to the world as a man with answers.
You are returning as a man who *knows how to stay in the question.*
Who no longer needs to be right to be whole.

This is the Sacred Masculine—not because he is above,
but because he is **in right relation with all things**.

He stands beside the Feminine—not behind, not ahead.
He honors the Earth—not as a resource, but as a temple.
He holds his lineage—not with bitterness, but with clarity.
He moves toward conflict—not with violence, but with vision.

Embodiment Practice: The Sovereign Stance

Exercise: The Axis of Presence

- Stand barefoot on the Earth. Eyes closed.
- Feel your spine—crown to root—align with the axis of the planet.
- Inhale as if breathing from the Earth.
- Exhale as if extending your energy skyward.
- Speak aloud:

> *"I no longer perform. I stand."*
> *"I no longer shrink. I serve."*
> *"I no longer seek power. I am aligned with it."*

Let your body remember what your mind cannot teach.

Reflection Ritual: Journal Inquiry

1. What does the Sacred Masculine feel like in me—not just as a concept, but as an energy?
2. Where do I still seek validation instead of moving from inner truth?

3. What sacred responsibilities am I ready to carry—not as burden, but as honor?

4. What would it mean to live as a man whose presence is his leadership?

Integration Oracle: The Crown Returns

"You are not here to dominate. You are here to bless."
"You are not here to win. You are here to align."
"You are not here to ascend. You are here to embody."

Let the crown settle not on your head,
 but in your spine.

Let your presence speak louder than your words.
 Let your love guide more than your logic.
 Let your power come from how you listen,
 and your legacy from how you live.

You are the man the world was waiting for—
 not because you've arrived,
 but because you've *returned* to what you've always been.

EMBODIED LEADERSHIP AND ENERGETIC INTEGRITY

Threshold Invocation: When Your Presence Becomes the Leadership

This is not about becoming a leader.
This is about **remembering that you already are one—**
because every step you take now echoes far beyond your own life.

You no longer lead through performance.
You lead through **frequency**.

When you walk into a room, the field shifts.
When you speak, it is from depth.
When you choose, it is from clarity.

Welcome to **Embodied Leadership and Energetic Integrity**.

This is the ring of kings.
Not the kings who rule by decree—
but the ones whose **being is their offering**.

The Misunderstanding of Leadership

Most models of masculine leadership are still built on hierarchy:

- Loudness mistaken for strength.

- Control mistaken for vision.
- Strategy mistaken for wisdom.
- Performance mistaken for presence.

But real leadership begins the moment a man becomes **non-reactive, energetically clean, and internally anchored**.

You do not lead by asserting yourself over others.
You lead by being **so congruent within**
that others naturally find clarity around you.

This is not charisma.
This is coherence.

Energetic Integrity Defined

Energetic integrity means:

- Your actions match your intentions.
- Your words are rooted in embodiment, not just ideas.
- Your nervous system is not outsourcing stability to others.
- Your leadership is clean—**free of subtle extraction, emotional manipulation, or unspoken agendas**.

It is the ability to:

- Say "yes" without people-pleasing.
- Say "no" without defensiveness.
- Hold power without becoming addictive to it.
- Guide without performing authority.

This is not perfection.
This is *alignment in motion*.

You Are No Longer Leading from the Head

The head plans.
The body knows.

The old masculine leadership model taught us to:

- Strategize before sensing.
- Move fast to avoid feeling.
- Lead others without leading ourselves.

But now, you are no longer the man who needs a map.
You are the man who *is becoming the compass*.

Embodied leadership means your decisions don't arise from impulse—
they arise from **resonance**.

You don't lead to be followed.
You lead because **you are in right relationship with life.**

Symbolic Activation Point #13: Leadership as Field

You are now the **field**—not just the force.

Others will begin to entrain to you.
Not because of what you say.
But because of what you *hold*.

This is when:

- Your silence becomes an anchor.

- Your "no" becomes a blessing.

- Your boundaries become medicine.

- Your presence becomes permission.

This is not egoic power.
It is **energetic hygiene**.

And it is holy.

The Five Traits of Embodied Masculine Leadership

Let these become internal postures—ways of being, not roles to perform.

1. Clarity

You speak the truth even when it costs you comfort.
You do not explain. You reveal.

2. Presence

You stay. When others collapse, react, or flee—you remain.
Not with rigidity, but with grounded love.

3. Coherence

Your energy is consistent across spaces.
You are not different men in different rooms.

4. Consent

You do not lead what does not want to be led.
You honor autonomy, even when it challenges your ego.

5. Transmission

You carry a frequency that speaks louder than your voice.
You've done the work. And now, **you are the work**.

What You Radiate Becomes the Teaching

You don't need to convince anyone of your power.
You don't need to project certainty.

You simply need to **live in full energetic truth**.
From that space:

- Your love teaches.//
- Your gaze initiates.
- Your discipline calibrates.
- Your actions become prayer.

This is **masculine service without saviorism**.
This is **power without performance**.
This is **leadership without egoic need**.

And this is the Masculine the world has been starving for.

Embodiment Practice: Field Alignment

Exercise: Energy Before Action

Before any significant action—conversation, decision, boundary—ask yourself:

- *Am I clean in my energy?*
- *Am I seeking to control, or to connect?*
- *Is this coming from truth, or strategy?*

Then breathe into your body.
Let your spine align.
Feel your energy **before you act.**

Only then, move.
Let presence lead before words arrive.

This is field leadership.

Reflection Ritual: Journal Inquiry

1. Where am I still leading from unprocessed fear, urgency, or ego?

2. What does energetic integrity mean for me in daily life and relationships?

3. Where have I confused charisma or control with true leadership?

4. How would my leadership shift if I trusted my body's wisdom first?

Integration Oracle: The Sovereign Speaks

"I no longer lead to be seen. I lead because I am aligned."
"My presence is a transmission. My truth is my offering."
"The field I hold shapes the world I live in."

You are no longer a man trying to lead.

You are now a man who *cannot help but lead*—
because you are coherent, rooted, and **in sacred relationship with your power**.

This is embodied leadership.
And it is what you were born for.

PURPOSE AS DEVOTION

Threshold Invocation: The Flame Beneath the Why

This is the moment you stop asking,

> "What am I supposed to do?"
> and begin asking,
> "What am I here to serve?"

This is not about ambition.
Not about legacy.
Not about being seen.

This is where **purpose becomes devotion.**

Not as a task,
but as a **prayer made visible through your life**.

You are not here to chase impact.
You are here to become a vessel
for something greater than your ego,
stronger than your doubt,
wiser than your fear.

This is **soul work**, brother.
And you are ready.

The Collapse of Purpose as Performance

For most of your life, "purpose" may have meant:

- Finding a mission.

- Building a vision.

- Making money doing something meaningful.

- Proving your value through your output.

This model turns purpose into productivity.
It turns your calling into currency.
It turns your soul's wisdom into a marketing plan.

But now—after all you've burned through—
you can finally see:
That wasn't purpose. That was survival wrapped in story.

You don't *find* purpose.
You **become available to it.**

True Purpose Is Not Found. It Is Remembered.

The masculine psyche seeks direction.
But the awakened masculine soul seeks **alignment**.

True purpose:

- Moves through you, not toward you.
- Arises from devotion, not desire.
- Is revealed through surrender, not control.

Purpose is not what you do.
It's what **you can't not do**
once you remember who you are.

It lives at the intersection of:

- Your deepest wound.
- Your greatest gift.
- The world's unspoken need.

And it only becomes clear
once the veils of performance, fear, and validation have fallen.

Symbolic Activation Point #14: You Are Not the Source. You Are the Vessel.

Let this rewire everything you've believed about purpose:

> *"My purpose is not mine to own. It is mine to serve."*

This is where you stop trying to "build a brand"
and start letting **your essence become a transmission**.

Your gifts are not achievements.
They are offerings.

Your path is not a career arc.
It is a **sacred agreement** with the soul of the world.

You are not the creator of this purpose.
You are the **guardian of it.**

The Masculine as Devotional Channel

The Sacred Masculine doesn't wake each morning asking,

> "What do I get today?"

He asks:

> "What am I here to serve?"
> "What field do I stabilize?"
> "What beauty do I protect?"
> "What truth do I anchor?"

This is devotion.

It is not soft.
It is not passive.
It is the **strongest stance a man can take**.

Because devotion is what keeps you moving
when reward is nowhere to be found.

It is what sharpens your discipline
and softens your heart—simultaneously.

When Purpose Hurts

There will be days when purpose feels heavy.
 When you question if it's working.
 When no one claps.
 When the world seems deaf to your offering.

Good.

Because this is when your purpose becomes **real**.

Purpose that doesn't break you at least once
 is probably still built on ego.

But the purpose that humbles you,
 that asks for more presence than you think you have,
 that takes you to your edge and brings you back clean—

That is the one worth giving your life to.

Embodiment Practice: Devotion in the Body

Exercise: Bow Without Words

- Find a quiet space. Kneel or sit in reverence.
- Place your hands on the earth, or your chest.
- Breathe slowly. Let your breath become an offering.
- Speak inwardly or aloud:

"I offer myself to what is real."
"Use me in service of what heals, awakens, and remembers."
"May my actions reveal devotion."

Then sit in silence.
Not asking.
Just listening.

Your purpose doesn't need to be found.
It just needs space to speak.

Reflection Ritual: Journal Inquiry

1. What have I believed about purpose that is ready to collapse?

2. Where has my pursuit of purpose been rooted in proving, not devotion?

3. What part of me already knows what I'm here to serve—but has been afraid to admit it?

4. If I were to let my soul lead… what would become non-negotiable in my life?

Integration Oracle: Purpose Speaks

"I do not need you to chase me. I need you to become still enough to hear me."
"I do not promise comfort. I promise meaning."

"You are not here to be impressive. You are here to be in service."

This is where your path begins to rise beneath your feet.
 Not because you forced it—
 but because you stopped blocking it.

Purpose is not found in the mind.
 It's heard in the heart.
 And walked out with **every sacred step you take in alignment**.

You are not here to save the world.
 You are here to serve the part of it that only *you* can reach.

And that, brother, is enough.

THE MASCULINE IN SERVICE TO LIFE

Threshold Invocation: You Are Not the Center—You Are the Channel

You've remembered your power.
You've reclaimed your sovereignty.
You've stopped performing and started listening.

Now the question becomes:

> *What is all this for?*

And the answer is not more success.
Not more mastery.
Not more approval.

The answer is simple.
Sacred.
Undeniable:

> **"I am here to serve life."**

This is the **final axis of embodiment**—
when the Masculine stops seeking what he can take,
and begins *becoming what life can move through.*

This is **Masculine Devotion in Motion.**

Beyond Mission: Becoming a Steward

Service is not a brand.
 It's not a role.
 It's not something you add to your life when you've "figured it out."

It is a **way of being**.

To be in service is to become a **guardian of life's intelligence**.
 Not to control it, but to **protect its sacred unfolding**.

You do not lead the river.
 You protect its source.
 You keep it clean.
 You walk its banks with reverence.

This is not theoretical.
 It is *embodied spiritual responsibility*.

True Service Begins When There Is Nothing Left to Prove

You don't serve to be seen.
 You serve because your **integrity demands it.**

The false masculine asks:

> "What do I get?"
> The sacred masculine asks: "What can I hold?"
> "What needs my presence, not my ego?"
> "Where am I being invited to become the space where love and structure meet?"

This is **service as embodiment**—
where your nervous system, attention, and values become an offering.

And you don't need applause.
Because your soul already knows:

> "This is what I was made for."

Service Is Not Always Grand—It Is Always Aligned

Service doesn't always look like leading a movement.
Sometimes it looks like:

- Holding space when your partner falls apart.

- Choosing presence over distraction with your child.

- Speaking truth in a room where silence keeps the peace.

- Refusing to abandon your body during conflict.

- Practicing right relationship with the Earth, even when no one's watching.

True service often goes unseen—
because it doesn't seek attention.
It seeks **coherence with life itself**.

Symbolic Activation Point #15: The Masculine as Stabilizing Force

You've collapsed your false thrones.
You've burned the performance mask.
You've integrated love and leadership.

Now you are called to **stabilize the field**.

This is the energetic function of the Sacred Masculine:

- To create structures that protect the Feminine flow.

- To offer clarity without control.

- To be consistent—not because you're rigid, but because you're reliable.

- To move with discernment—not urgency.

You are no longer just a man.
You are a **pillar**.

Not above.
But **within**.
Grounded.
Clear.
Alive.

You Become the Environment

This is the highest masculine transmission:

> *Your very being becomes a permission slip for others to return to themselves.*

You walk into the room,
and something softens.

Not because you *do* anything—
but because you're **no longer fragmented**.

You've remembered how to carry power without proving.
And now, the field responds to your coherence.

This is **energetic legacy**.
This is **service through presence**.

Embodiment Practice: Aligning with Life

Exercise: Listening for the Assignment

- Sit in stillness. Breathe into the question:
  "What is life asking of me right now?"

- Not *what do I want*.

- Not *what should I do*.

- But:
  "Where is life already moving through me that I've been ignoring?"

When the answer comes, don't argue.
Don't dramatize.

Just say:

> "I accept this assignment."
> "I offer myself as a vessel."

Then act. Small or large.
That is service.

Reflection Ritual: Journal Inquiry

1. What does service mean to me beyond achievement or obligation?

2. Where is life inviting me to step forward with devotion—not ego?

3. What spaces in my world need my presence more than my opinion?

4. What is one consistent practice I can offer in devotion to life, without needing reward?

Integration Oracle: Life Responds

"You are no longer here to consume life. You are here to consecrate it."
"Let your breath be prayer. Let your touch be guidance. Let your presence be sanctuary."

"Wherever you go, let others feel more human because of your coherence."

You are not here to serve a god outside of you.
You are here to serve the divine *through you*.
Through how you lead.
How you love.
How you show up.

You are now a vessel of life's unfolding.
Let it move through your words,
your actions,
your boundaries,
your stillness.

This is not sacrifice.
This is sovereignty in service.

Chapter 6: BROTHERHOOD AND THE SACRED CONTAINER

This path was never meant to be walked alone.

You were taught to compete.
To compare. To outperform.

But deeper than all of that is something older:
The circle.
The mirror.
The silent "I see you" between men who have nothing left to prove.

This chapter dissolves isolation.
It collapses the myth of masculine separation.
It reawakens the truth:

You are not alone.
You were never meant to be.

Threshold Invocation: The Circle You Were Never Meant to Walk Without

You were not meant to do this alone.

Even if you were taught to.
Even if you learned to trust no one.
Even if you became so good at holding it all that you forgot what it's like to be held.

This is the threshold of **Brotherhood**—
but not the kind built on banter, bravado, or surface loyalty.

This is the **Sacred Container**.
Where men gather not to fix each other,
but to remember themselves—**together**.

What Brotherhood Really Means

Brotherhood isn't about similarity.
It's about **shared presence in truth**.

In its sacred form, brotherhood is:

- A space where masks drop first.

- A space where competition dies.

- A space where another man's power doesn't threaten yours—it *activates* it.

- A space where your grief, your laughter, your anger, your edge all belong.

It is not group therapy.
It is **collective remembrance.**

Why Men Need a Sacred Container

Because isolation breeds distortion.
And disconnection from other men becomes a **disconnect from self**.

When you're alone too long:

- You begin to believe your shadows are uniquely shameful.

- You mistake survival strategies for personality.

- You normalize dysregulation.

- You forget that your pain doesn't make you weak—it makes you human.

But when another man sits beside you, unmoved by your emotion,
unshaken by your truth,
and says,

"I've been there. I'm not leaving,"

something ancient reawakens.

This is **initiation through shared witnessing**.

Applied Example: What Brotherhood Looks Like

Let's ground this:

You're in a circle.
A man speaks his edge—his anger at his father, his fear of failing his family.
His voice cracks.
There's no rush to comfort.
No jokes to defuse it.

Just space.

Another man breathes with him.
Another one nods—wordless recognition.
One speaks:

> "You're safe here. You don't need to carry this alone."

No one fixes.
No one flinches.

That moment is the container.
That's where transformation happens.

Not in theory.
In presence.

The Energetic Blueprint of the Sacred Container

There are 3 qualities that differentiate a sacred circle from a casual gathering:

1. Non-Performance

You do not need to impress.
 You only need to arrive as you are.

2. Co-Regulation

Your nervous system recalibrates by being in the presence of grounded men.
 This is **real, biological healing**.

3. Witnessing Without Control

You are seen—fully, fiercely, without being managed or corrected.

In these spaces, you're not just remembering who you are.
 You're remembering who you *never stopped being*, beneath the cultural noise.

Inclusivity Note: Brotherhood as Archetype, Not Exclusion

Let's clarify:
 "Brotherhood" in this text doesn't mean *only men, only one kind of man, only this language*.

It means the field of **energetic resonance** that forms when people agree to:

- Show up raw.

- Drop performance.

- Reflect each other's wholeness without projection.

For some, this is a men's circle.
 For others, it's a conscious partnership, a primal mentorship, a father-child bond, or a chosen tribe.

The word is "brotherhood,"
 but the frequency is **homecoming**.

Symbolic Activation Point #16: The Circle as Portal

A sacred container isn't just a gathering.
 It's a **portal into higher relational consciousness**.

Every time you sit in circle:

- You collapse hierarchy.

- You metabolize trauma through witnessing.

- You remember how to feel *with others*.

- You shed the illusion of "I'm the only one."

In myth, men gathered in caves, at fires, on mountain trails.

Now we gather in backyards, Zoom rooms, gyms, breathwork tents.

But the fire is still here.
And you're being called to sit beside it—*not someday, now.*

Embodiment Practice: Call the Circle

Exercise: Create the Container

- Reach out to one man this week—someone you respect, or someone you know is struggling.

- Don't ask how he's doing. Ask:

  "What's real for you right now?"

Then **listen without fixing**.
Hold silence. Hold breath. Hold space.

This is brotherhood in motion.
It doesn't need ceremony.
It just needs **courageous presence.**

Reflection Ritual: Journal Inquiry

1. When was the last time I let another man see me without a mask?

2. What keeps me from fully entering spaces of masculine connection?

3. What kind of brother do I long to be—and what kind of brother have I been?

4. Who in my life is waiting for an invitation into deeper presence?

Integration Oracle: The Circle Speaks

"You were never meant to carry this alone."
 "Let yourself be known—not when you've healed, but as you heal."
 "The fire you're looking for is already lit. You just need to take your seat."

There is a kind of healing you cannot access in solitude.
 There are thresholds that only open when **walked beside others.**

You don't need to lead the circle.
 You don't need to know what to say.

You just need to show up
 and stay.

INITIATION THROUGH BROTHERHOOD

Threshold Invocation: When One Man Crosses, We All Feel It

There comes a moment when a man steps forward—
not for himself,
but for the collective.

He breaks silence.
He owns his story.
He weeps without apology.
He forgives his father.
He confesses the lie he built his life upon.
He tells the truth he thought would exile him.

And when he does,
something ancient cracks in every other man present.

This is **Initiation Through Brotherhood**.

Not a solo descent.
Not a rugged individual odyssey.

But a **shared becoming**.

This is what happens when men stop mirroring each other's masks
and begin mirroring each other's *truth*.

The Nature of Relational Initiation

Most men think initiation is solitary:

- Vision quests.
- Plant medicine journeys.
- Solo breakdowns.
- Quiet rebirths.

These are sacred.
But incomplete.

There are initiations you cannot walk alone.
Because they **don't require isolation—they require reflection**.

Relational initiation means:

- Letting another man hold the mirror when you can't see yourself.
- Hearing your story spoken from someone else's mouth.
- Feeling your pain rise as someone else speaks *what you were too afraid to say*.

And in that moment, you realize:

"*It was never just me.*"

Why Brotherhood Is a Crucible

In the presence of real brotherhood:

- You can't hide as easily.
- You can't fake your healing.
- You can't shrink into isolation.
- You can't rely on performance.

You are **called forward by example**.

When another man risks honesty,
 you feel your own integrity rise to meet him.

That's not competition.
 That's coherence.

Brotherhood is a **field**, not a role.
 And when one man steps through the veil,
 it pulls every other man closer to his own threshold.

Applied Example: The Moment Everything Changes

You're in circle.
 A man begins to speak—his voice shaking.
 He shares that he's been carrying a secret:
 porn addiction, father rage, self-hatred, numbness in his marriage.

He says it aloud—shame pulsing through every word.

And then something happens:
No one flinches.
No one looks away.
No one tries to fix him.

Instead, another man says:

> "Thank you. You just said the thing I haven't been able to admit."

And suddenly, *four other men nod.*

The field shifts.
Truth becomes contagious.
And what was once hidden becomes holy.

This is initiation through collective witnessing.

Masculine Alchemy: Fire Needs Fire

Masculine energy expands not just through solitude, but through **friction and reflection**.

In a true brotherhood:

- One man's clarity becomes another's compass.

- One man's rage becomes another's permission.

- One man's surrender becomes another's softening.

- One man's devotion becomes another's recalibration.

We rise together not in *unison*, but in **resonance**.

Like iron sharpening iron.
Like flame awakening flame.

This is not codependence.
This is **co-activation**.

The Archetypal Function of Initiatory Brotherhood

Initiatory brotherhood fulfills what modern culture stripped away:

- The **rites** that marked the shift from boy to man.

- The **elders** who mirrored your gifts without coddling your illusions.

- The **men** who held your rage without fear.

- The **tribe** who said, "We see you. Keep going."

When men create this for one another—
they don't just heal their own lineages.
They heal what their fathers never had access to.

This is **lineage alchemy**.
This is **intergenerational repair**.

And you're not just a participant.
You are a **portal for it to happen again.**

Symbolic Activation Point #17: You Are a Living Threshold

There will be a moment when you realize:

> *"It's not just about me anymore."*

Your healing activates others.
Your integrity steadies others.
Your softness invites others.
Your presence **becomes the initiation** for men who've never had one.

You become the field.
You become the mirror.
You become the mentor without having to perform it.

And that?
That's when you've crossed into **relational maturity**.

Embodiment Practice: Mirror of the Circle

Exercise: Reflective Witnessing

- Sit with one man—friend, brother, partner, colleague.

- Agree to share 2–3 minutes each, uninterrupted, on the question:

> "What is something real I haven't been saying out loud?"

- The listener's task is not to fix, solve, or comment.
- Only to hold eye contact.
- When finished, simply say:

"I see you. Thank you."

Then switch.

Let the field speak more than your commentary.

Reflection Ritual: Journal Inquiry

1. When have I experienced another man's truth becoming my initiation?
2. What part of me still hesitates to be seen by other men?
3. What would it mean to create spaces where men can meet themselves?

4. Who in my circle is already ready to walk deeper—if only I go first?

Integration Oracle: The Circle Deepens

"You do not need to be healed to sit in the circle. You only need to be willing."
"You are not just here to be witnessed. You are here to become a mirror."
"Let your threshold be the one others remember crossing."

Brotherhood is not a luxury.
 It is **a biological, psychological, and spiritual necessity.**

It is the fire that reveals what solitude cannot.
 It is the forge where the sacred masculine is remembered.

And when you take your place inside that container,
 you're not just entering circle.

You're becoming part of a lineage that will carry this medicine
 for generations.

FROM COMPARISON TO COHERENCE

Threshold Invocation: The Moment You Stop Measuring

What if you no longer needed to compare?

What if another man's power didn't threaten yours—
 but clarified it?

What if success wasn't a race,
 but a rhythm you remembered?

This is the veil that holds so many in quiet war with themselves:

Comparison.
 The reflex to measure your value
 by the surface expressions of others.

But you are standing at the edge now.
 The place where **competition dissolves**
 and coherence begins.

Comparison Is Not Conscious—It's Conditioned

You didn't choose to compare.
It was installed early.

You learned it in classrooms and locker rooms.
In the subtle glances between fathers and sons.
In the way success was praised and softness punished.

You were told:

- Be faster.

- Be stronger.

- Be smarter.

- Be more.

And beneath all of it:

> "Be better than him."

Comparison became identity architecture.

And now...
you're invited to dismantle it.

What Comparison Really Does

It doesn't just steal joy.
 It fractures **connection**.

When you compare:

- You stop seeing the other man clearly.

- You measure his outside against your inside.

- You contract your energy instead of expanding it.

- You distort your own purpose by trying to wear someone else's skin.

The result?

Mutual distortion.
 Both men lose their center.

And brotherhood turns into shadow theatre.

Coherence: The Energetic Antidote

Coherence means:
 Your thoughts, emotions, body, and actions are **aligned**.

Not perfect.
 But true.

And in this state:

- You're less reactive to others' power.

- You don't need to win to feel worthy.

- You remember your unique rhythm, and stop outsourcing your pace.

When you're coherent, **comparison becomes irrelevant.**

You're no longer trying to match someone else's flame.
You're tending your own fire.

Applied Example: From Rivalry to Resonance

Imagine two men working side by side.

One speaks with clarity.
The other listens with depth.
One leads.
The other holds the field.
Neither tries to outshine.

They each know their frequency.
And because of that, they amplify each other.

This is coherence.
It's not sameness.
It's **complementarity**.

Like drum and bass.
Like sun and shadow.

You don't need to dim to belong.
You just need to **align**.

Symbolic Activation Point #18: From Mirror to Beacon

In comparison, the other man is a mirror for your insecurity.

In coherence, the other man becomes a **beacon**.

He doesn't trigger your wounding.
He reminds you of your **capacity**.

When you see his power, you feel your own return.

When you feel his clarity, it activates your own voice.

This is when men stop fragmenting each other
and start **recalibrating each other's nervous systems.**

This is **field intelligence** in motion.

Why This Matters for Brotherhood—and Beyond

When comparison collapses,

- Competition becomes collaboration.
- Envy becomes empathy.

- Judgment becomes curiosity.

- Rivalry becomes resonance.

This doesn't just change how you see other men.
It changes how you **relate to your own evolution**.

You stop chasing upgrades, and start deepening embodiment.

You stop rushing your purpose, and start **trusting its pace**.

And from this place, your leadership changes.
Your relationships change.
Your **entire field** becomes trustworthy.

Embodiment Practice: Field Realignment

Exercise: Anchor Your Signature Frequency

- Sit or stand. Breathe into your belly.

- Visualize another man in your life who evokes comparison.

- Notice the sensation—tightness, heat, contraction.

Now breathe into your **center**—your own energy.
Let his frequency fall away.

Ask yourself:

> "What is my unique rhythm?"
> "What truth lives in me that no one else carries?"

Speak aloud:

> "I do not need to match him. I need to remember me."

Repeat until your breath deepens.
Until you feel **yourself return.**

Reflection Ritual: Journal Inquiry

1. Who do I compare myself to, and what part of me feels threatened by them?

2. What am I afraid I'll never become—and is that fear even mine?

3. What is one way I can anchor into coherence instead of seeking validation?

4. What becomes possible in brotherhood when I stop needing to be "more"?

Integration Oracle: The Mirror Softens

"You were never meant to be him. You were meant to be coherent."
"Let his light remind you, not reduce you."

"You do not need to outrun anyone. You only need to remember your rhythm."

This is the end of fragmentation.
This is the end of hierarchy.
This is the birth of **energetic respect.**

When men become coherent,
they don't just stop competing—
they start *amplifying each other's missions.*

And that...
changes the world.

THE FIELD OF THE INITIATED MAN

Threshold Invocation: When You Are No Longer Just a Man—You Are a Field

You've crossed the thresholds.
You've burned the masks.
You've spoken the truths.
You've stopped performing and started embodying.

Now something deeper is emerging—
not just *within* you, but **around** you.

You are no longer only a man with presence.
You are becoming a **field of resonance**.

What you've integrated doesn't just live in your choices—
it lives in your **energetic signature.**

This is what it means to become an **initiated man**:

> You carry a field that *reminds others who they are—*
> without having to say a word.

What Is "The Field"?

The field is the invisible space your body, energy, and integrity create.

It is not mystical fluff.
It is biological.
Relational.
Spiritual.
Archetypal.

People feel it:

- In the **nervous system regulation** you radiate.

- In the **safety** they sense in your presence.

- In the way your **truth steadies** a room.

- In the **non-reactivity** you hold during chaos.

- In the way you don't flinch when life gets real.

The field of the initiated man is not about perfection.
It's about **coherence + containment + clean power**.

It's a *frequency of trust*.

What Changes in the Field of the Initiated Man

Once you embody this field:

- You no longer need to fix others—they regulate just by being near you.

- You don't need to over-explain—your presence transmits clarity.

- You stop absorbing projections—you metabolize them.

- You don't need to control outcomes—your alignment shapes them.

- You become **safe to challenge, soft to witness, strong to stand**.

You don't perform healing.
You radiate it.

This is not symbolic.
This is **initiation embedded in your biology.**

Applied Example: The Field at Work

You walk into a space where tension is thick—unspoken conflict, fractured communication.

You say little.
You sit, breathe, stay grounded.

And slowly:

- The volume of anxiety decreases.

- People begin speaking more truthfully.
- Emotions rise—then settle.
- Someone breaks the silence… honestly.

What happened?

You held the field.

Not with words.
With *coherence*.

And the others felt permission to do the same.

This is the field of the initiated man at work:
Not as dominator. Not as savior.
As **stabilizer. Amplifier. Mirror.**

Why the World Needs This Field Now

Because we are in a collective field **fractured by nervous system dysregulation**, ego inflation, and spiritual bypass.

The initiated man becomes a **living countercurrent**.

He anchors:

- Depth in shallow spaces.
- Stillness in overstimulated rooms.

- Truth in fragmented cultures.
- Connection in the age of performance.

He doesn't fight the distortion.
He simply *becomes the clarity* within it.

And over time, *he entrains the field around him.*

This is **real energetic leadership.**
This is what changes systems from the inside out.

Symbolic Activation Point #19: From Initiate to Anchor

You are no longer walking *into* initiation.
You are now walking *as* it.

You carry:

- The descent.
- The fire.
- The witnessing.
- The grief.
- The rebirth.
- The integration.

You've touched the mythic.
Now you become the myth-maker.
Not through story—but through **embodied signal.**

Every step is transmission.
Every boundary is calibration.
Every choice is frequency work.

You are now a field.
And the field is **alive in you.**

Embodiment Practice: Radiant Presence Transmission

Exercise: Becoming the Field

- Sit in stillness. Upright spine. Eyes closed.

- Inhale slowly through the nose, exhale longer through the mouth.

- Visualize your field expanding 2–3 feet beyond your body.

- Breathe coherence into it.

- Ask silently:

    "Who am I when I'm not protecting or performing?"
    "What does the world feel when it enters my presence?"

- Say aloud:

"I am the signal. I am the stabilizer. I am the flame."

Let this presence expand, not from force—
but from **full internal permission**.

Reflection Ritual: Journal Inquiry

1. What happens to people in my presence—and what does that tell me about my field?

2. Where am I still sourcing my identity from effort instead of energy?

3. What would it mean to lead through resonance, not reaction?

4. Who in my life is already shifting—simply because I've become more coherent?

Integration Oracle: The Field Speaks

"You are not here to dominate the room. You are here to stabilize it."
"You are not here to speak the loudest. You are here to echo the deepest truth."

"Let your presence be the altar. Let your life be the initiation."

You are no longer just a man.
You are a field of coherence.
A signal of truth.
A container for transformation.

You will not need to announce it.
You will not need to be chosen.

Your embodiment will speak for itself.

Chapter 7: LIVING THE INTEGRATION

You're not here to talk about what you've remembered. You're here to live it.

This is where everything gets real.
Not in the ritual.
In the repetition.

Not in the breakthrough.
In the repair.

This chapter is not a crescendo. It's a continuation.
It's where you learn how to carry the sacred into your morning routine.
Into your conflict. Into your commitments.

The fire no longer needs to burn around you.
Because now, it burns within you.

Threshold Invocation: The Return to the Village

You've walked the fire.
You've spoken the silence.
You've held your own gaze without flinching.
You've stepped beyond the boy, the mask, the performance.

Now the final rite begins:

Can you bring it home?

This is where many initiations lose their power—
not because the descent failed,
but because the return was never integrated.

You are not here to stay in the sacred cave.
You are here to **live the sacred in the ordinary.**

This is **Living the Integration**—
where the myth becomes muscle,
where presence meets the grocery store,
where truth is lived *in the middle of life*.

The Return Is the Real Test

It's one thing to feel powerful in a circle.
To speak truth with brothers around the fire.
To cry beneath the stars in the arms of a guide.

But what happens:

- When your child is screaming?
- When your partner is triggered?
- When the world isn't soft, spiritual, or supportive?
- When the sacred isn't seen or celebrated?

That's where integration begins.

Not when it's convenient—
but when your nervous system wants to reach for the old pattern
and you choose presence instead.

Not because it's easy—
but because it's **who you are now.**

What Integration Really Means

Integration isn't about maintaining a state.
It's about **building capacity**.

To live the truth you remembered in moments of expansion
even when contraction returns.

Integration means:

- Choosing the slower, more conscious breath.
- Saying the honest "no" before resentment builds.

- Returning to the body when the mind tries to escape.
- Listening fully before responding.
- Repairing ruptures before they calcify.

It means **bringing the sacred into the space between breakfast and bedtime.**

Applied Example: Sacred in the Mundane

You're tired.
Your partner is upset.
A younger version of you wants to defend, deflect, fix, or flee.

Instead, you pause.
You breathe.
You say:

> "I'm here. I hear you. Let's slow down."

Not because it's perfect.
Not because it's easy.
But because **you're no longer willing to abandon presence**.

You just brought the sacred into a Tuesday night argument.
That is integration.

What Will Try to Pull You Back

You will be tempted to regress.

Old habits.
 Old crowds.
 Old rhythms that make you forget who you've become.

That doesn't mean you've failed.
 It means **you're being tested at the integration layer.**

The world may not validate your transformation.

So you must become the man
 who no longer needs external mirrors
 to stay connected to internal truth.

Symbolic Activation Point #20: The Sacred Walks With You Now

You no longer need ritual to remember.
 You've become the ritual.

You no longer need fire to awaken.
 You've become the flame.

Your breath is now the practice.
 Your attention is now the devotion.
 Your boundaries are now the altar.

This is the final embodiment:
 Not when the world sees your change—
 but when *you live it anyway.*

Key Integrative Anchors for Daily Life

Let's ground this now.

◆ 1. Rituals Over Routines

Even brushing your teeth can become an act of presence.
Let your mornings include one conscious breath, one grounding thought, one clear intention.

◆ 2. Micro-Alignments

Catch the subtle reactions—defensiveness, withdrawal, people-pleasing.
Interrupt the pattern with breath and truth.

◆ 3. Transparent Repair

You will make mistakes.
Integration means **repairing cleanly, without shame or retreat.**

"I spoke from fear. I want to reconnect."
Simple. Sovereign.

◆ 4. Body First, Strategy Later

Let the body guide your choices.
If it contracts, pause.
If it expands with stillness, trust.

Embodiment Practice: Sacred Re-entry

Exercise: Anchor in the Ordinary

- Choose one daily act—making coffee, showering, driving, email.
- Before beginning, pause.
- Place a hand on your heart. Inhale deeply.
- Say silently:

"This, too, is holy."

Let your pace slow by 10%.
Let your breath deepen.
Let your posture speak:

"I carry the sacred in every moment now."

Repeat daily.
The mundane becomes mythic when you bring your full presence.

Reflection Ritual: Journal Inquiry

1. Where in my daily life do I abandon the man I remembered myself to be?

2. What old identities still whisper to me when I'm tired, rushed, or triggered?

3. What would it feel like to let my relationships reflect my integration, not just my intentions?

4. What are three ways I can bring sacredness into the next 24 hours?

Integration Oracle: The Sacred Speaks Softly Now

"I am not waiting for you at the next retreat. I am beside you in every breath."
"Do not chase the fire. Become the hearth."
"Live your truth when no one is watching—that is the sign of the initiated."

You are no longer chasing breakthrough.
You are now *building embodiment*.
Quietly. Steadily. Sovereignly.

Let others wonder how you became this clear,
this kind,
this grounded.

You won't need to explain.
Your presence will be enough.

STAYING ROOTED IN THE STORM

Threshold Invocation: The Storm Doesn't Break You—It Builds You

There will be pressure again.

The world won't soften just because you've awakened.
There will be moments when everything you've remembered will be tested by chaos, confusion, or conflict.

But this time...
you won't collapse.
Because you're no longer trying to avoid the storm—
you are learning to **anchor inside it.**

This is the final gift of integration:

Stability that holds even when nothing else does.

Not because life is calm—
but because *you are.*

The Masculine Root System

The Sacred Masculine is not defined by dominance.
He is defined by **depth**.

Like a tree, he grows by going down before reaching up.

Your root system is:

- Your breath.
- Your values.
- Your integrity.
- Your nervous system regulation.
- Your capacity to stay when the storm wants you to run.

Most men were taught to endure storms by tensing.
But you now learn to **open into the pressure**.

That's not fragility.
That's *energetic resilience*.

What the Storm Reveals

In the storm, the following will be tested:

- Do your boundaries hold—without aggression?
- Do you speak the truth—even when it's inconvenient?
- Can you stay emotionally regulated—even when others are not?

- Can you receive another's pain without collapsing or fixing?

The storm doesn't come to punish you.
It comes to **reveal where your roots are shallow.**
Where you're still outsourcing safety.
Where you're still bracing instead of breathing.

This is the kind of pressure that doesn't destroy you—
it **refines** you.

Applied Example: Rooted in Relationship Conflict

You're in an argument with your partner.

Your pulse rises.
Your chest tightens.
Your old reflex wants to interrupt, defend, distance.

But instead…

You pause.
You feel your feet.
You breathe through your belly.
You listen.

Then you speak—not to win, but to stay true:

> "I feel the urge to shut down, but I want to stay connected. I'm here."

That moment *is the storm.*
And *you just became the anchor.*

This is not just spiritual.
It's **practical, relational mastery.**

Symbolic Activation Point #21: Breath as the New Backbone

When the wind rises, your thoughts will race.
Old stories will return.
Your nervous system will beg to self-protect.

But your breath is your root.

Inhale: return to the now.
Exhale: let go of control.
Inhale: come back to center.
Exhale: speak from coherence.

You no longer need to armor up.
You only need to **drop in**.

Your power is no longer reactive.
It is **anchored.**

Storm Types: Recognize, Respond, Root

Let's ground this:

◆ **1. Emotional Storms**

Triggered grief, unresolved rage, sudden vulnerability.

Stay rooted by:
Naming the emotion. Feeling the body. Slowing your breath.

> "This is anger. This is grief. I can feel it without fusing to it."

◆ 2. Relational Storms

Conflict, projection, rupture, misunderstanding.

Stay rooted by:
Listening fully. Speaking from the body. Leading with repair.

> "Let me make space for this. We'll find our way."

◆ 3. External Storms

Job loss. Uncertainty. Global crisis. Loss of direction.

Stay rooted by:
Returning to daily practice. Serving something bigger. Staying consistent.

> "I don't need clarity to act with integrity."

Embodiment Practice: Rooting in Pressure

Exercise: Simulated Storm

- Sit. Bring to mind a real situation that creates pressure.
- Let your body feel it. Let the emotion rise.
- Do not analyze. Do not fix. Just *breathe*.

Now speak aloud:

> "I can hold this."
> "I don't abandon myself here."
> "The storm is welcome. I remain."

Let your spine remain long.
Let your feet stay grounded.
This is your energetic root system in action.

Reflection Ritual: Journal Inquiry

1. What storms tend to pull me off center?
2. What coping strategies have I outgrown, but still reflexively use?
3. What anchors (practices, values, breathwork) bring me back when I'm spinning?
4. What would it mean to trust myself even when the storm is loud?

Integration Oracle: The Storm Speaks

"I did not come to destroy you. I came to test what you've built."
"I am not the enemy. I am the mirror."
"When you remain present in me, you become unshakable."

Storms will continue.
Life will stretch you.
Pressure will rise.

But now…
you are different.

Not because you're invincible.
But because you no longer **leave yourself when things get hard.**

You stay.
You soften.
You root.

And because of that,
you rise.

INTEGRATION AS LEGACY

Threshold Invocation: What You Carry Forward Becomes the World

You've walked the descent.
You've remembered the man beneath the mask.
You've reclaimed truth, anchored in storm, chosen presence.

Now, the final shift unfolds:

> **You are no longer just integrating for yourself.**
> You are becoming the *living bridge* between what was and what will be.

This is **Integration as Legacy**.

Not legacy as achievement.
Not legacy as empire.
Legacy as **energetic inheritance**.

What you embody now becomes what others **inherit— energetically, emotionally, archetypally.**

This is the masculine as *transmitter*, not just transformer.

Legacy Is Not What You Leave Behind— It's What You Carry Forward

Legacy isn't stored in history books.
It's carried in:

- The nervous systems of your children.

- The unspoken safety others feel around you.

- The relational patterns you rewrite.

- The presence you model without performance.

- The quiet *"I see you"* you offer to the next man on the edge.

**Legacy lives through how you live,
 not just what you leave.**

And every step you take now is sending signals down your lineage.

Applied Example: Embodiment as Transmission

You're in a moment with your child, your partner, your student, your younger brother.

They're upset. Confused. Disconnected.

You don't lecture.
 You don't withdraw.
 You breathe.

You stay.
You model what regulation looks like.

You say:

> "It's okay to feel this. I've been here too. Let's find the breath together."

That moment...
is generational change.

You just gave them a template they didn't have before.

That's legacy in real time.

From Individual Breakthrough to Collective Repair

You are not healing in isolation.

Every pattern you collapse,
 every reaction you deprogram,
 every truth you speak,
 becomes a ripple in the masculine field.

Because:

- Your son will grow up not fearing his own tears.

- Your daughter will recognize what grounded love feels like.

- Your partner will learn to trust the consistency of the masculine.

- Your community will calibrate to your coherence.

This is how **cultural myths dissolve.**
Not through theory.
Through *embodied modeling*.

Symbolic Activation Point #22: You Are a Living Lineage Shift

You don't just represent yourself.
You carry:

- The wounds your father didn't know how to name.

- The longing your grandfather buried.

- The rage your brother misdirected.

- The brilliance your uncle never voiced.

And now—
you choose to carry it **cleanly**.

You become the man who:

- Integrates instead of inherits.

- Transmits healing instead of trauma.
- Offers safety where there was once silence.

You are not here to fix your lineage.
You are here to **rewrite its trajectory**.

Legacy Is in the Daily, Not the Dramatic

Your legacy lives in:

- The text you send instead of disappearing.
- The apology you speak without defense.
- The breath you take before reacting.
- The boy you mentor on the basketball court.
- The space you hold in a fatherless friend's grief.
- The boundary you set without resentment.

You don't need to build an empire.

You just need to **become the man your lineage never had—**
 and now does.

Embodiment Practice: Ancestral Transmission

Exercise: Root → Now → Reach

- Sit in stillness. Imagine three generations behind you. Men who never spoke what you've now spoken.

- Place your hands over your heart and say:

    "You didn't fail. You didn't know. I see you. And I carry it differently now."

- Now imagine three generations ahead—children, mentees, collective future men.

- Speak:

    "What I integrate now becomes your freedom."

Let the weight shift from burden to **blessing.**

You are the pivot point.
You are the lineage anchor.

Reflection Ritual: Journal Inquiry

1. What patterns am I interrupting that were normalized in my family or culture?

2. What does legacy mean to me now, beyond status or success?

3. Who is already being impacted by my integration—and how can I honor that?

4. What do I want the men who come after me to feel in their bones, because of the man I became?

Integration Oracle: Legacy Whispers

"You are the bridge. You are the repair."
"They may not remember your name. But they will feel your freedom."
"Let your life whisper to the future: 'We did not stay asleep.'"

You are no longer walking alone.
Your integration is being echoed behind you.

And in front of you,
a future is forming—
not from force,
but from the quiet radiance
of a man who stayed the path
when no one was clapping, but everything was shifting.

This is your legacy.

This is your echo.

This is the long breath of becoming.

THE PATH AHEAD

There is no arrival—only deeper return.

*What you've walked through does not make you special.
It makes you responsible.*

*Not for being perfect.
But for staying present.*

*Let your life become the ritual.
Let your choices become the altar.
Let your presence become your prayer.*

*The path continues.
Walk it true.*

Threshold Invocation: There Is No Ending—Only a New Way of Walking

You've crossed the fire.
You've shattered the mirror.
You've breathed your way back into your own center.

And now...
 the question returns:

> "What now?"

Not with urgency.
 Not with pressure.

But with **deep presence.**

You do not need a grand plan.
 You need only to **walk forward with the man you've become.**

This is **The Path Ahead**—
 not a prescription, but a permission.

To live, lead, love, and rise
 from your truth.
 From your coherence.
 From your embodiment.

Not just for you—
 but for **everyone you're now a mirror to.**

The Path Is Not Linear—It Spirals

The work isn't over.
 It never is.

But now you understand:

- Healing isn't a destination—it's a rhythm.

- Presence isn't a peak—it's a practice.
- Power isn't dominance—it's devotion.
- Masculinity isn't performance—it's embodiment.

You'll revisit the same lessons.
 But each time, from deeper stillness.
 More self-trust.
 More grace.

This spiral is sacred.
 It means you're alive.
 It means the path is still unfolding beneath your feet.

And you're no longer running.
 You're **walking with intention.**

The Man You Are Now Knows How to Begin Again

You don't need to fear forgetting.
 Because now you know how to remember.

You've built rituals.
 You've rooted in breath.
 You've trusted your voice.
 You've honored your body.

So when you fall again (and you will),
 you'll rise faster.

Softer.
Wiser.

This is the real integration:
**Not avoiding collapse—
but walking through it cleanly.**

Let the Sacred Be Normal Again

You don't need to be intense to be deep.
You don't need to be stoic to be strong.
You don't need to be "spiritual" to be sacred.

Let your path be honest.
Let your love be direct.
Let your joy return.

Be the man who laughs easily
because he has nothing to prove.
Be the man who still weeps
because he has nothing to hide.

The sacred is not a separate space.
It is in the **way you live the ordinary.**

Applied Integration: Let Your Life Speak

The initiated man doesn't talk about his journey all the time.
He doesn't need to.

Instead, he:

- Moves slower in rooms of urgency.
- Stands taller when the crowd wavers.
- Breathes deeper when emotion rises.
- Chooses alignment over applause.
- Lets love change him again and again.

He walks as a field,
not as a performance.

And the people around him—
even if they don't understand why—
begin to feel safer.

Symbolic Activation Point #23: You Are the Spiral Now

You are not at the end.
You are at the *center*.

The spiral turns now around you.
Each action ripples.
Each truth echoes.
Each pause radiates.

You are the man who stopped running from his shadow.
The man who let fire burn away what wasn't real.
The man who came back to the village different—
not louder, but clearer.

This is the completion that begins again.

And again.
 And again.

Embodiment Practice: The Living Breath

Exercise: Remembering Forward

- Sit in silence. Eyes closed.

- Place one hand on your heart. One on your belly.

- Ask:

    "What part of me am I bringing forward with reverence?"
    *"What part of me am I leaving behind with love?"
    "What truth is asking to be lived now?"

Breathe.
 Listen.
 Then rise and walk forward—
 not into performance,
 but into presence.

Reflection Ritual: Journal Inquiry

1. Who have I become—not in title, but in tone, presence, and energy?

2. What am I most proud of shifting, forgiving, or facing?

3. What is one way I can support other men now—not by teaching, but by *living it out loud*?

4. What will my life now transmit to those who walk beside or behind me?

Final Oracle: The Masculine Path Is Alive in You

"You do not need to strive. You need to remember."
"You do not need to finish. You only need to walk."
"You do not need to be more. You only need to be true."

This is not the end.

This is the breath before the next moment.
The pause between impact and echo.
The calm clarity before the next spiral opens.

Walk from here with your shoulders down,
your breath low,
your heart visible.

And if you forget—
come back.

If you fall—
 come back.

If you rise—
 bring others with you.

This is your path now.

And you are ready.

EPILOGUE

No One Can Walk This For You Now

There will be no final lesson here.
 No grand conclusion.
 No flourish of words to wrap the spiral.

Only this:

> You have remembered enough
>   to begin living differently.

And that is everything.

You won't always feel clear.
You won't always stay centered.
You won't always make the aligned choice in the moment.

But now—
you'll notice when you don't.
You'll return faster.
You'll know the way back.

Because the man you are now
can feel when he's left himself.

And more importantly—
he knows how to come home.

There is no map for what comes next.

No perfect practice.
No single lineage.
No ten-step model to keep you safe from the next unraveling.

But you don't need a map anymore.
Because you're no longer trying to escape the unknown.

You're walking with it.

Your breath is your anchor.
Your presence is your compass.
Your choices are your offering.
Your life is your rite.

You will fall.
You will forget.
You will ache.

But you will **remember faster.**
You will **stay longer.**
You will **speak clearer.**
You will **love harder.**
You will **breathe deeper.**

And that, my brother, my friend,
is what changes everything.

Let the world wonder what shifted in you.

You won't need to explain.

Your life will say enough.

Walk gently.
Stand clearly.
And when the next threshold appears—

Step through.

You're ready.

I do not need applause.
I do not need understanding.
I do not need to be named.

I only need to walk—
with breath in my belly,
and the sacred in my spine.

I carry no teachings, only presence.
No perfection, only permission.
No answers—just the discipline to stay in the question.

I am the one who returned.
Not louder.
Not more enlightened.
Just clearer.
More here.

I do not fear the dark anymore.
I've learned to see in it.

I do not rush to love.
I *become* it.

I speak less.
I anchor more.

And when the next boy asks,
"Is it possible to live without the mask?"

I will look him in the eye
and say nothing.

He'll feel it.
And that will be enough.

Letter from the Author

To the Reader—

You may wonder—why *Veil Origins*?
Why now?
Why this path?

The answer doesn't live in theory. It lives in the ache behind the noise. The fracture behind the performance. The absence behind the armor.

Because something sacred has been missing—
Not quietly. Violently.
Not by accident. But by design.

What's been missing is the true Sacred Masculine.

Not the image of control we were handed.
Not the myth of dominance or the silence we inherited.
But the original current—devotional, grounded, protective.
A Masculine that doesn't conquer the world…
But holds it.

This book is not written to glorify manhood.
It's written to *redeem* it.

It's not about reclaiming power as status.
It's about restoring power as *presence*.

It's not about going back.
It's about going *deeper*—to what was exiled, and must now return clean.

We live in a world where men are either feared or forgotten.
Where boys are expected to become men with no elders, no

rites, no mirrors.
Where performance replaced purpose, and disconnection became identity.

This book is where that ends.

But make no mistake—this book is not just for men.

It's for anyone who feels the ache of the missing Masculine.
Anyone who has longed for a strength that doesn't dominate, a clarity that doesn't control, a presence that *remembers*.

Because the suppression of the Feminine wounded the world.
But so did the distortion of the Masculine.
And healing cannot come through blame.
It comes only through **Sacred Union**—within and without.

I didn't write this to speak for all men.
I wrote it to speak to the man I once was—
The one who wore the mask so long, he forgot there was a face beneath it.
The one who called numbness strength, and silence peace.
The one who didn't know what he was missing… until the ache cracked him open.

This book is an initiation.
A funeral and a remembering.
A mirror held up to the fire.

And yes—this book is the mirror to *Beyond the Veil: A Journey to Feminine Freedom*.
They are not separate. They are a twin flame code.
Two currents. One union.

Because Feminine freedom cannot fully return unless the Masculine rises beside her.

Not in performance. In *presence*.
Not in domination. In *devotion*.

If you are a man reading this—I honor the courage it takes to stay open.
If you are a woman reading this—I honor your power to call us forward, not as rivals, but as mirrors. As equals. As necessary halves of a greater whole.

We are not waiting for healing.
We *are* the healing.

It begins here—
With breath.
With fire.
With truth.

With you.

In fierce reverence,

Don L. Gaconnet
☐ *Author of Veil Origins: A Modern Rite of Passage for Men* ☐

www.ingramcontent.com/pod-product-compliance
Lightning Source LLC
Chambersburg PA
CBHW050554170426
43201CB00011B/1691